OLD TESTAMENT GUIDES

COLLEGE LIBRARY

**Please return this book by the date stamped below
- if recalled, the loan is reduced to 10 days**

Fines are payable for late return

HOSEA

Graham I. Davies

Sheffield Academic Press

First Published by Sheffield Academic Press 1993

Copyright © 1993, 1998 Sheffield Academic Press

Published by Sheffield Academic Press Ltd
Mansion House
19 Kingfield Road
Sheffield S11 9AS
England

Printed on acid-free paper in Great Britain
by The Cromwell Press
Trowbridge, Wiltshire

British Library Cataloguing in Publication Data

A catalogue record for this book is available
from the British Library

ISBN 1-85075-393-8

Contents

Preface

In this short introduction to Hosea I have tried to take account of recent developments in the study of the prophets without losing sight of older contributions to the subject which have stood the test of time. The topics dealt with are those with which an undergraduate student of theology who knows no Hebrew could be expected to become familiar. For that reason the difficult text-critical problems of the book are not covered here: reference should be made to the larger commentaries for a treatment of them. The order of the chapters is designed to bring the reader as quickly as possible to the prophet's teaching (Chapter 2), with various subordinate (but important) issues being treated later. Biblical quotations are taken from the New Revised Standard Version, except for a few places, mainly in Chapter 7, where I have given a translation of my own to make a particular point clearer.

There are a number of places in the book of Hosea where the chapter-divisions occur at different points in the Hebrew text and in English translations. Similar variations exist elsewhere in the Old Testament. Throughout this book I have followed the verse-numbering of the English versions, and in Hosea the following equivalences should be borne in mind when consulting the Hebrew original:

Eng. tr.	1.10-11	=	Heb.	2.1-2
	2.1-23	=		2.3-25
	11.12	=		12.1
	12.1-14	=		12.2-15
	13.16	=		14.1
	14.1-9	=		14.2-10

I am most grateful to Professor Norman Whybray, the editor of the series, for his careful review of the manuscript of this book and his helpful comments and advice, and to my son Peter, who has again acted as a most efficient typist.

G.I. Davies

Abbreviations

ANET	J.B. Pritchard (ed.), *Ancient Near Eastern Texts*
ATD	Das Alte Testament Deutsch
AV	Authorised Version
BASOR	*Bulletin of the American Schools of Oriental Research*
BJRL	*Bulletin of the John Rylands Library*
BZ	*Biblische Zeitschrift*
BZAW	Beihefte zur Zeitschrift für die Alttestamentliche Wissenschaft
CBC	Cambridge Bible Commentary
DOTT	D.W. Thomas (ed.), *Documents from Old Testament Times*
ET	English Translation
EVV	English Versions
ICC	International Critical Commentary
JBL	*Journal of Biblical Literature*
JSJ	*Journal for the Study of Judaism*
JSOTSup	*Journal for the Study of the Old Testament* Supplement Series
KAT	Kommentar zum Alten Testament
NCB	New Century Bible
NEB	New English Bible
NRSV	New Revised Standard Version
OBO	Orbis Biblicus et Orientalis
OTL	Old Testament Library
OTS	Oudtestamentische Studiën
PEQ	*Palestine Exploration Quarterly*
REB	Revised English Bible
SBLDS	Society of Biblical Literature Dissertation Series
TLZ	*Theologische Literaturzeitung*
TOTC	Tyndale Old Testament Commentary
VT	*Vetus Testamentum*

Commentaries on Hosea

Modern commentaries available in English include:

W.R. Harper, *Amos and Hosea* (ICC; Edinburgh: T. & T. Clark, 1905). A classic commentary, with the strengths and the weaknesses of the early phase of modern biblical criticism. A mine of information about linguistic and textual matters.

G.A.F. Knight, *Hosea: God's Love* (Torch Bible Commentary; London: SCM Press, 1960). A brief early example of a more theological approach to the book.

J.M. Ward, *Hosea: A Theological Commentary* (New York: Harper & Row, 1966). A valuable work of exegesis, which discusses earlier scholarship in a thorough but readable way.

J.L. Mays, *Hosea* (OTL; London: SCM Press, 1969). A very readable commentary which is still a valuable guide to the prophet's thought.

H. McKeating, *The Books of Amos, Hosea and Micah* (CBC; Cambridge: Cambridge University Press, 1971). Clear and effective in conveying the results of modern scholarship in a limited space.

H.W. Wolff, *Hosea* (Hermeneia; Philadelphia: Fortress Press, 1974) (ET of German original [Biblischer Kommentar], 2nd edn, 1965). A detailed modern treatment of all aspects of the book. Always worth consulting and particularly useful for word-studies, form criticism and Hosea's relationship to earlier tradition.

F.I. Andersen and D.N. Freedman, *Hosea* (Anchor Bible; Garden City, NY: Doubleday, 1980). Strong on stylistic aspects and metre, but often over-elaborate and unconvincing on matters of translation and textual criticism.

D. Stuart, *Hosea-Jonah* (Word Biblical Commentary; Waco, TX: Word Books, 1987). A determined effort to interpret Hosea against the background of the whole Pentateuchal covenant tradition, in conscious opposition to mainstream scholarship.

P.J. King, *Amos, Hosea and Micah: An Archaeological Commentary* (Philadelphia: Westminster Press, 1988). Not a commentary in the normal sense, but a series of studies which provide an invaluable source of background information.

D.A. Hubbard, *Hosea* (TOTC; Leicester: Inter-Varsity Press, 1989). A scholarly and sensitive explanation of the text, which sees it as entirely the work of Hosea.

G.I. Davies, *Hosea* (NCB; London: Harper Collins, 1992).

Four German commentaries which have not been translated into English are:

J. Wellhausen, *Die Kleinen Propheten* (Berlin: G. Reimer, 3rd edn, 1898, repr. de Gruyter, 1963).

A. Weiser, *Die Propheten Hosea, Joel, Amos, Obadja, Jona, Micha* (ATD; Göttingen: Vandenhoeck & Ruprecht, 1949, 6th edn, 1974).

W. Rudolph, *Hosea* (KAT; Gütersloh: Gerd Mohn, 1966).

J. Jeremias, *Der Prophet Hosea* (ATD; Göttingen: Vandenhoeck & Ruprecht, rev. edn, 1983).

1

HOSEA AND HIS TIME

THE BOOK OF HOSEA is unusual in the Old Testament in that it comes from the old northern kingdom of Israel before its downfall in 722 BCE. Despite a few later additions made after it had become part of the sacred prophetic literature of Judah, it in large measure retains its original 'northern' character. Jerusalem is never mentioned in its pages, and the royal line of David only once (3.5), in what most commentators now regard as an insertion into the older context. The many contemporary place-names in Palestine which Hosea mentions are, with one exception, all northern or eastern: Jezreel (1.4-5, 11; 2.22), Gilgal (4.15; 9.15; 12.11), Beth-aven/Bethel (5.8; 10.5, 8; 12.4), Mizpah (5.1), Tabor (5.1), Shittim (5.2), Gibeah (5.8; 9.9; 10.9), Ramah (5.8), Adam (6.7), Gilead (6.8; 12.11), Shechem (6.9), Samaria (7.1; 8.5-6; 10.5, 7; 13.16), Baal-Peor (9.10), Beth-arbel (10.14). The exception is the 'valley of Achor' (2.15), which lay on the border between the tribal districts of Judah and Benjamin (Josh. 15.7), and so was technically within the territory of the southern kingdom. But this is a special case, as the valley of Achor owed its significance not to contemporary events but to the tradition of Israel's entry into Canaan, as this is presented in the book of Joshua (see Josh. 7.24-26), and in fact to a part of that tradition (chs. 2–9) which is commonly seen as having originally been the special tradition of the tribe of Benjamin.

Hosea's northern roots are also evident in the fact that he mentions 'Ephraim' 36 times, nearly as often as 'Israel' (39 times), while the name 'Judah' only occurs 14 times, the majority of these references (though not all) probably being

Hosea

later additions to the text. Possibly also the use of a northern dialect could explain some of the peculiarities of the language of Hosea, but in the absence of comparable texts this is hard to prove. It is not possible to be certain about Hosea's exact place of origin. The biblical text gives no explicit statement on the matter, in contrast to certain other prophetic books (e.g. Jer. 1.1, Amos 1.1). The tradition that he came from the city of Ibleam, near modern Jenin (*Vitae prophetarum*: see Harper, *Amos and Hosea*, p. 202), is late and the rabbinic view that he was of the tribe of Reuben is based purely on the comparison of his father's name Beeri with the name of a place mentioned in 1 Chron. 5.6. It is possible that he was a native of the capital Samaria: this would explain his familiarity with matters of state, particularly in chs. 7–8 and 10, and perhaps also the fact that his place of origin is not stated—it may only have been thought necessary to mention this in the case of a prophet who was from outside the capital. Nothing is known of his occupation, though some clues will be mentioned in Chapter 5. The famous story of his marriage will need a chapter all to itself.

The troubled times in which Hosea lived and prophesied are, as with all the earlier prophets, an essential background for the understanding of his message. The details can be found in any of the modern histories of Israel (see the list at the end of this chapter), and only an outline need be given here. A broad indication of the period of Hosea's ministry is given in the opening verse of the book:

> ...in the days of Kings Uzziah, Jotham, Ahaz, and Hezekiah of Judah, and in the days of King Jeroboam son of Joash of Israel.

Since Jeroboam II died while Uzziah was still on the throne (cf. 2 Kgs 14.29; 15.8, where Uzziah is called by his other name Azariah), it is clear that a much fuller list is given here of the kings of Judah than of the kings of Israel under whom Hosea prophesied. This is no doubt due to the fact that the book as we have it was designed for Judaean readers, a fact of which there are other signs elsewhere in the book. The list of Judaean kings takes Hosea's activity down at least to the mid-720s BCE, and this is in line with some specific allusions to historical events in the book, which will be referred to below.

Jeroboam II died about 750 BCE (different chronologies place the event a few years before or after the middle of the century) and the six-month reign of his son and successor Zechariah marked the end of a dynasty which had held power in the northern kingdom of Israel for close on a century, ever since Jehu's bloody revolt and reformation (2 Kgs 9–10). After early troubles with the powerful kings of Syria, its kings had been able to make Israel a large and prosperous nation once more (2 Kgs 14.23-27; Amos 6), but the assassination of Zechariah was a sign of internal tension and further evidence of social divisions can be found in the book of Amos, who was active towards the end of Jeroboam's reign. Hosea himself spoke of the coming end of the dynasty in what is probably one of his earliest oracles:

> And the Lord said to him, 'Name him Jezreel: for in a little while
> I will punish the house of Jehu for the blood of Jezreel, and I will
> put an end to the kingdom of the house of Israel' (1.4).

No new dynasty was able to establish itself in Israel after the fall of the house of Jehu. Zechariah's murderer reigned for only one month before he was himself killed by Menahem, who then seized the throne (2 Kgs 15.14). He in turn was succeeded by his son Pekahiah, but after only a short reign he too was murdered; there was a military uprising with support from Gilead in Transjordan, whose leader, Pekah, then assumed the kingship (2 Kgs 15.25). The figure of twenty years given for his reign in 2 Kgs 15.27 cannot be right, and he may have ruled for only three or four years, before himself falling victim to a conspiracy which put Hoshea the son of Elah (not to be confused with the prophet) on the throne. Hoshea was the last of the kings of Israel; he was taken prisoner by the Assyrians shortly before the fall of his capital Samaria to them in 722/21 (2 Kgs 17.4). The precise chronology of these short reigns and of their Judaean counterparts is disputed at several points, but the following chart may serve for reference:

Israel	Judah	Assyria
Jeroboam II (787–745)	Uzziah (787-736)	
Zechariah (745)		Tiglath-Pileser III
Shallum (745)	Jotham (756-742)	(745–727)
Menahem (745–736)	Ahaz (742–727)	
Pekahiah (736–735)		
Pekah (735–732)		Shalmaneser V
Hoshea (732–723)	Hezekiah	(727–722)
	(727–698)	Sargon II
		(722–705)

For the modern historian, some help with these chronological problems comes from the fact that during these years the Assyrians suddenly became increasingly involved in the history of Israel and Judah; consequently a number of cross-references can be made between their royal inscriptions and Old Testament narratives and prophecies. From the point of view of the people of the time, this Assyrian involvement, first in Syria and then further south, was a major factor, probably the major factor, affecting royal policy and, indeed, the rapid changes of ruler in Israel. The dominant figure is Tiglath-Pileser III, also known as Pul, whose reign (745–727) probably matches the duration of Hosea's prophetic activity very closely. The most probable interpretation of Tiglath-Pileser's numerous and very successful military campaigns is that they were initially directed at stifling the influence of Assyria's northern neighbour Urartu on trade in Syria, but subsequently aimed at extending direct Assyrian control wherever local rulers were unwilling to accept or to remain loyal to treaty-conditions which recognized Assyrian hegemony. As far as Israel is concerned, we know both from the Old Testament (2 Kgs 15.19-20) and from Tiglath-Pileser's own annals that Menahem paid tribute to Assyria (*ANET*, p. 283; *BASOR* 206 [1972], pp. 40-42). Pekah, however, became involved in an anti-Assyrian coalition which included Philistia, Arabia, Damascus and other parts of Syria as well, and the famous attempt to force Judah into the coalition is referred to in Isaiah 7. Tiglath-Pileser was engaged in campaigns to suppress opposition from 734 to 732 and again both the Old Testament and his own inscriptions mention specifically the effects of these campaigns on Israel:

> King Tiglath-Pileser of Assyria came and captured Ijon, Abel-
> beth-maacah, Janoah, Kedesh, Hazor, Gilead, and Galilee, all
> the land of Naphtali; and he carried the people captive to Assyria
> (2 Kgs 15.29: compare *ANET*, pp. 283-284, *DOTT*, p. 53).

This reduced the kingdom to about a third of its former size.
All Galilee and Transjordan became provinces of the Assyrian
empire, many of the population were deported and only the
hills around Samaria were left as nominally independent.
Pekah was overthrown, and the new king Hoshea received
Assyrian approval in return for a resumption of the payment
of tribute (2 Kgs 15.30; *ANET*, p. 284, *DOTT*, p. 55). Some
have thought that Psalm 80 reflects the popular reaction to
this catastrophe.

Hoshea's loyalty to Assyria was, however, apparently not
unshakeable, and when Tiglath-Pileser's reign came to an
end with his death in 727, he apparently made a bid for independence. At least this seems to be implied by the statement
that 'King Shalmaneser [Tiglath-Pileser's successor] came up
against him; Hoshea became his vassal, and paid him tribute'
(2 Kgs 17.3). Further support for this view may possibly lie in
a text from the Babylonian Chronicle which is usually associated with the final destruction of Samaria but can more appro-
priately be related to the year 727 according to N. Naaman.
This text reads:

> The second year [sc. of Tiglath-Pileser III's rule in Babylon]...
> On the twenty-fifth day of the month Tebet Shalmaneser (V)
> ascended the throne in Assyria <and Akkad>. He ravaged
> Samaria (*probable reading*).
> --
> The fifth year: Shalmaneser (V) died in the month Tebet.
> (trans. A.K. Grayson)

Resistance to Shalmaneser early in his reign may have been
widespread, as there is also evidence, in a Tyrian chronicle,
that the Phoenician city of Tyre came under attack (cited in
Josephus, *Antiquities*, 9.283), and in a recent article J.K. Kuan
has suggested that this event is referred to in the somewhat
obscure Hos. 9.13:

> Ephraim, just as I have seen Tyre planted in a pleasant place,
> so Ephraim must lead his children out to the slaughterer.

The oracle against Philistia in Isa. 14.29-32 may also belong
here. Some of Hosea's other sayings seem to imply that
already at that time the states of the Levant were looking to
Egypt for support in their anti-Assyrian stance (7.11, 16). This
is specifically said to have been the case when, some three
years later, Hoshea again challenged Assyrian hegemony by
refusing to pay tribute (2 Kgs. 17.4). To judge from the
account of the Assyrian counter-measures, it seems that
neighbouring kingdoms joined in the resistance on this occasion: Tyre (according to Josephus, cited above), the Philistine
city of Ashdod and a place called Shinuḫtu (*ANET*, pp. 284-
85; *DOTT*, pp. 60-62). The hope of help from Egypt was a
vain one, as Egypt was anything but a united kingdom at this
time: the Nile delta alone was divided into several different
princedoms. The most likely identification of 'So, king of
Egypt' in 2 Kgs 17.4 is with Osorkon IV, ruler of Tanis in the
north-eastern delta, whose forebears had had good relations
with the northern kingdom of Israel in the ninth century.

It is implied in 2 Kgs 17.4-5 and 18.9-10 that it was
Shalmaneser V who both captured Hoshea, leaving Israel
under the rule of elders or courtiers, and initiated the siege of
Samaria. No annals of Shalmaneser survive, and the only
possible reference outside the Bible to action by him is the
passage in the Babylonian Chronicle referred to above. The
surviving Assyrian evidence ascribes the capture of Samaria
to Sargon II, who succeeded Shalmaneser at the end of 722
(*ANET*, pp. 284-85; *DOTT*, pp. 59-60). One of these texts
begins with an obscure reference to another king, but
whether this is Shalmaneser or an ally of Samaria is not clear.
It then continues:

> not to do service and not to bring tribute...and they did battle. I
> clashed with them in the power of the great gods, my lords, and
> counted as spoil [2]7, 280 people together with their chariots...
> and the gods in whom they trusted. From among them I
> equipped 200 chariots for my royal army units, while the rest of
> them I made to take (up their lot) within Assyria. I restored the
> city of Samaria and made (it) more habitable than before. I
> brought into it people from the countries conquered by my own

hands. My official I set over them as district-governor and reckoned them as people of Assyria itself (Nimrud Prism, 4.25-41; *DOTT*, p. 60).

There is a close correspondence between this and the account in 2 Kings 17. In view of Hosea's polemics against idolatry, it is especially interesting that Sargon refers to 'the gods in whom they trusted', by which images are probably meant. Another inscription places the capture of Samaria 'at the beginning [of my rule]', that is, in Sargon's accession year. Both because of this and because Sargon's annals refer to them as separate events, the Assyrian capture of Samaria is to be distinguished from the participation of Samaria in a revolt in Sargon's second full year (i.e. 720/719), which appears to have been organized from the Syrian city of Hamath, but involved Damascus, Gaza, Egypt and other peoples as well. Recently it has been suggested by H. Tadmor and N. Naaman that Sargon only attacked Samaria in the context of the revolt led by Hamath in 720, but this is not what his inscriptions say and it is probably mistaken to telescope what are reported as two very different events. There appears to be no reference in the Old Testament to the second episode, but it may have involved only a few diehards.

The excavations at Samaria carried out by the Harvard Expedition (1908–10) and the Joint Expedition (1931–35) have brought to light evidence of the splendid architecture and fortifications of the Israelite city and also of its devastation by the Assyrians. A layer of ash covered its ruins, and in this were found many fragments of carved ivory, relics of the exotic decoration of the royal palace. A display of the latter can be seen in the City Museum at Birmingham. Remains of buildings from the period of Assyrian rule which began in 722 are much more sparse but three interesting finds are a fragment of a cuneiform stele, probably from the reign of Sargon II, an inscribed Assyrian cylinder seal, and a cuneiform legal document which mentions a local governor with the name Avi-aḥi. Other cuneiform texts, from Nimrud, show that some of the captured Samarians were enrolled in the Assyrian chariot forces.

Further Reading

For recent general accounts of Hosea's historical background see:

A. Malamat (ed.), *The Age of the Monarchies: Political History* (The World History of the Jewish People, IV.1; Jerusalem: Massada Press, 1979), pp. 44-60 (chronology), 180-91 (history from 745 to 721).

S. Herrmann, *A History of Israel* (London: SCM Press, 2nd edn, 1984), pp. 233-54.

J.A. Soggin, *A History of Israel* (London: SCM Press, 1984), pp. 217-31.

J.M. Miller and J.H. Hayes, *A History of Ancient Israel and Judah* (London: SCM Press, 1986), pp. 307-39.

The translation of the Babylonian Chronicle on p. 17 is taken from:

A.K. Grayson, *Assyrian and Babylonian Chronicles* (Locust Valley, NY: J.J. Augustin, 1975), p. 73.

The possible references to an Assyrian attack on Tyre in 727 are discussed in:

J.K. Kuan, 'Hosea 9.13 and Josephus, *Antiquities* IX, 277-287', *PEQ* 123 (1991), pp. 103-107.

On archaeological evidence see:

P.J. King, *Amos, Hosea and Micah: An Archaeological Commentary* (Philadelphia: Westminster Press, 1988).

A. Malamat (ed.), *The Age of the Monarchies: Culture and Society* (The World History of the Jewish People, IV.2; Jerusalem: Massada Press, 1979), pp. 187-204, 225-35 (general), 237-78 (crafts, industry, houses, tombs).

2

A SKETCH OF HOSEA'S TEACHING
AND ITS DEVELOPMENT

THE BOOK OF HOSEA is undoubtedly best known for the 'story of Hosea's marriage' with which it begins (chs. 1–3) and for the way in which the symbolism of a marriage and its break-down is used there to portray the love of God for his people and his reaction to their unfaithfulness in turning to the worship of Baal. This is unfortunate for two reasons. First, it has given undue prominence to debates about the exact sequence of events in Hosea's relationships: are the women in chs. 1 and 3 the same or different? If the same, do the two chapters refer to separate incidents or do they in part overlap? What kind of woman exactly was Gomer? Answers to these questions have often been the basis for attempts to explain the origin or the purpose of Hosea's teaching. But, as the very existence of such different theories shows, the evidence in these chapters is insufficient to enable Hosea's biography to be written with any certainty, and this is clearly not the purpose with which the chapters were put together. Some consideration will be given to these problems in this book, but it seems advisable to defer this until more important matters have been dealt with.

The second reason why exclusive concentration on the first three chapters is to be regretted is that it tends to promote an account of Hosea's teaching which is both unbalanced and foreshortened. Careful study of the teaching and background of the sayings in chs. 1–3 suggests that they actually origi-nate, like the sayings in the remainder of the book, not from a short, formative episode in Hosea's life but from the full

extent of his long prophetic activity (1.1). They have been
separately edited on the basis of their themes and imagery
and placed at the beginning of the book to give prominence to
those themes and that imagery. Exactly when this happened
is no longer clear but it is probably significant that it is the
teaching of these chapters of the book which was most influential on later prophets such as Jeremiah, a fact that suggests
that already in his time (c. 600 BCE) they may well have been
given their present prominent place. There is even some evidence that Hosea himself may have given some impetus to
this synthesis of one strand of his teaching (see below on ch.
2). But to understand the full breadth of his teaching and to
grasp its revolutionary handling of the traditions and institutions of Israel it is necessary to look at the contents of these
chapters along with those that follow them in the book. In
fact, to counterbalance the influence which chs. 1–3 have had
on previous perceptions of Hosea, there is much to be said for
looking first at chs. 4–14.

Hosea's Criticism of his Contemporaries

Chapter 4 opens immediately with a statement that Yahweh
has an accusation to bring against his people Israel. This is
expressed first negatively, in terms of certain qualities that
are missing from their life:

> There is no faithfulness or loyalty,
>   and no knowledge of God in the land (4.1).

The absoluteness and generality of these charges is to be
noted: Hosea is not speaking only about particular individuals
who have failed to display the customary virtues of community life, but of a society in which they are no longer
present at all. 'Faithfulness' (*'emet*) and 'loyalty' (*ḥesed*, elsewhere translated 'steadfast love', as in 6.6) are qualities of the
widest possible application in human relationships: they refer
to truthfulness and honesty, such as is expected of judges
(Exod. 18.21), and to a readiness to respond generously with
help to a fellow human being in need, such as a member of a
family which has fallen on hard times (2 Sam. 9.1). Often the
two qualities are mentioned together as summing up one's

obligations to one's fellows (e.g. Gen. 24.49) or indeed the way in which God himself was believed to deal with mankind (e.g. Ps. 25.10). Thus far, then, Hosea is lamenting the abandonment of traditional Israelite values in the society of his day. But he connects this with an absence of 'knowledge of God', which is a much rarer expression in the Old Testament but one which is particularly common in this book (cf. 2.20; 4.6; 5.4; 6.3, 6: cf. 2.8; 11.3; 13.4). It was clearly of special importance to him and should be a vital clue to the nature of his teaching. What did it mean?

It appears to have been an expression used in the public prayers of Hosea's day: 'Israel cries to me, "My God, we—Israel—know you!"' (8.2). There it was simply a way of expressing the special bond, as between intimate friends, that was believed to exist indissolubly between Israel and their God. Some commentators have thought that it has the same sense for Hosea, so that his words would imply simply that there was no longer any real intimacy between Israel and Yahweh. This is, however, an example of the way in which too much concentration on Hosea 1–3 can lead to a distortion of the prophet's real teaching. Hosea's own understanding of the notion was much more specific, as the following verses in Hosea 4 suggest (cf. 11 and 14 as well as 2 and 6). In the first place, it is no coincidence that in v. 2 the prophet turns immediately to list a series of sins which may be intended to spell out what the absence of knowledge of God means. It has frequently been noted that three of the words used in this catalogue—murder, stealing and adultery—correspond exactly to the language of the Decalogue or 'Ten Commandments', so that the prophet could be seen as rebuking the people for their transgression of the law. Although some recent scholarship has associated the composition of the Decalogue very closely with the production of the book of Deuteronomy a century and more after Hosea, it remains likely that the Deuteronomists took over an already existing summary of Yahweh's demands, which may already have been known in the time of Hosea. Certainly a few verses later Hosea is complaining that the people's ruin is due to a failure of the priests to teach 'the law of your God' (v. 6: cf. 8.1, 12),

and here what is rejected is specifically referred to as
'knowledge', a term which it is hardly possible to dissociate
from the 'knowledge of God' mentioned earlier.

One component of 'knowledge of God' thus seems to be a
knowledge of and obedience to the divine law. But that is not
all. As H.W. Wolff pointed out, there are also places in Hosea
where Israel's lack of 'knowledge of God' is seen in what can
best be described as their forgetfulness of Yahweh's provision
for their needs in the past:

> She *did not know* that it was I who gave her
>   the grain, the wine and the oil,
> and who lavished upon her silver
>   and gold that they used for Baal (2. 8).

> Yet it was I who taught Ephraim to walk,
>   I took them up in my arms;
> but they *did not know* that I healed them (11.3).

Sometimes Hosea uses the very word 'forget' in his accusations (2.13; 4.6; 13.6; 8.14 may be a later addition).
'Knowledge of God' for Hosea therefore presupposes a respect
for specific traditions about history and law; and this is an
understanding of the expression which can be traced in both
earlier and later writings in the Old Testament (cf. 1 Sam.
2.12; 3.7; Isa. 5.12-13; Jer. 31.34). To understand it in this
way is not of course to reduce religion to an acceptance of a
series of propositions, and Hosea himself lays considerable
emphasis elsewhere on the breach of the relationship between
Israel and Yahweh that has occurred. In addition to the very
clear evidence in chs. 1–3 (see below), this is particularly evident in 8.2, which links disobedience to the law with the
breaking of the covenant, in 6.7, where covenant-breaking is
paralleled by faithlessness, and in 5.7, where the latter notion
appears again.

The next feature to emerge, however, is that Hosea's
sayings pick out the priests and the politicians of his day for
special criticism. In so doing he was setting himself up against
the two most powerful institutions in ancient Israelite
society—the network of shrines throughout the country and
the royal court with the king at its centre. We have already
noted how he criticized the priests for failing to teach the law

of God to the people. His attack on them continues in 4.7-10, where he accuses them of having sunk so low that they actually encourage the people in 'sin' so that they, in their growing numbers, can live off the profits. Apparently Hosea has in mind the practices of sacrifice, divination, cultic prostitution and idolatry which he goes on to list in the remainder of the chapter (vv. 10, 12, 13, 14, 17-19) and to which he repeatedly refers as 'whoredom' (vv. 11, 12, 15). A further look at what Hosea was criticizing here and the reasons for it will be found in a later chapter. But the priesthood is also attacked for its involvement with politicians and their intrigues (5.1-3; 6.7-10). These matters constitute a much more central theme of Hosea's preaching than one might suppose from reading chs. 1–3. His preaching includes criticism of particular actions and policies in both external and internal affairs, but there is also a very radical questioning of the very legitimacy and permanence of the political institutions themselves. Again further attention to this theme will be required in another chapter, and we must be content with some examples here.

Hosea repeatedly criticizes, and even mocks, the foreign policy of Israel's rulers, as they seek support from the great powers of the day, Assyria and Egypt.

> When Ephraim saw his sickness,
>   and Judah his wound,
> then Ephraim went to Assyria,
>   and sent to the great king.
> But he is not able to cure you
>   or heal your wound (5.13).

> Ephraim has become like a dove,
>   silly and without sense;
> they call upon Egypt, they go to Assyria (7.11).

> For they have gone up to Assyria,
>   a wild ass wandering alone;
> Ephraim has bargained for lovers (8.9).

> Ephraim herds the wind,
>   and pursues the east wind all day long;
> they multiply falsehood and violence;
>   they make a treaty with Assyria
>   and oil is carried to Egypt (12.1).

But it will all be in vain:

> They shall not remain in the land of the Lord;
>> but Ephraim shall return to Egypt,
>> and in Assyria they shall eat unclean food (9.3).

> For even if they escape destruction,
>> Egypt shall gather them,
>> Memphis shall bury them (9.6).

As for events at home, an obscure passage, 6.7–7.7, speaks
of internal strife, assassination and *coups d'état*, summed up
as 'the corruption of Ephraim' and 'the wicked deeds of
Samaria', the northern capital (7.1). Contrary to what royal
propaganda may be presumed to have asserted—since it did
so in every other state of the ancient Near East, including
Judah—the king and his court were not, Hosea says, divinely
appointed and divinely protected: they were at the mercy of
their enemies:

> They made kings, but not through me;
>> they set up princes, but without my knowledge (8.4).

> Samaria's king shall perish,
>> like a chip on the face of the waters (10.7).

> At dawn the king of Israel shall be utterly cut off (10.15).

> Where now is your king, that he may save you?
>> Where in all your cities are your rulers,
> of whom you said,
>> 'Give me a king and rulers'?
> I gave you a king in my anger,
> and I took him away in my wrath (13.10-11).

Judgment and Hope in Hosea

The account of parts of Hosea's teaching given in the past few
pages may well cause surprise for another reason, namely its
severity. Within chs. 4–14 there is very little indication that
Israel can hope for any further blessing from Yahweh: in fact,
apart from 5.15–6.3, 10.12, 11.8-11, 14.1-8, the expected
outcome is exclusively of judgment, and comprehensive and
brutal judgment at that. In addition to passages already
quoted we may note such statements as:

For I will be like a lion to Ephraim,
  and like a young lion to the house of Judah.
I myself will tear and go away;
  I will carry off and no one shall rescue (5.14).

Now he will remember their iniquity,
  and punish their sins;
  they shall return to Egypt (8.13).

The threat of a 'return to Egypt' was an especially shocking prospect, since it meant the turning back of history beyond the celebrated deliverance from Egypt at the exodus and a return to 'the house of bondage'.

Ephraim is stricken,
  their root is dried up,
  they shall bear no fruit.
Even though they give birth,
  I will kill the cherished offspring of their womb.
Because they have not listened to him,
  my God will reject them;
  they shall become wanderers among the nations (9.16-17).

This predominant note (at least as far as quantity is concerned) of condemnation and judgment has to be taken fully into account if a true picture is to be given of Hosea's prophetic message. But this is, as we have seen, not the whole story, even in chs. 4–14. There are occasional glimpses of the possibility and even the certainty of a better future. We can best approach this topic by way of an examination of one final major feature of Hosea's message of judgment: his exposition of the history of his people as a history of sin.

More even than other prophetic books, the book of Hosea is full of allusions, sometimes rather obscure, to both recent and much earlier history (cf. 5.1-2, 10; 6.7-9; 9.9, 15; 10.9, 14; 12.11-13; 13.11). But from the middle of ch. 9 onwards there is a series of passages which all begin with a 'historical retrospect' and which convey a clear and consistent prophetic perspective on the nation's past history, and these can be both compared and contrasted with those which we encounter in the historical books and in certain psalms (e.g. Ps. 78). The obvious difference is that Hosea's perspective is not expounded in a single narrative; rather he uses powerful images to bring into sharp focus the religious significance of the past as he understood it.

The *Leitmotif* of these passages is the damning contrast between Yahweh's initial delight in Israel and his care for them at the beginning of their history, on the one hand, and on the other their own lapse into idolatry and corruption after the settlement in Canaan. In the first such passage (9.10) the original attractiveness of Israel is expressed in two images drawn from the natural world, before the prophet passes on to an allusion to a story of apostasy at the very entry into the land of Canaan (cf. Num. 25):

> Like grapes in the wilderness
> > I found Israel.
> Like the first fruit on the fig tree in its first season,
> > I saw your ancestors.
> But they came to Baal-peor,
> > and consecrated themselves to a thing of shame,
> > and became detestable like the thing they loved.

What Hosea is saying is that the present corruption of Israel's social and religious life, with its consequent loss of divine favour, is something deeply rooted in their history, and that therefore the judgment that is threatened in the following verses is fully deserved.

A similar view is expressed in 10.1-2. Israel enjoyed abundant fruitfulness in the land, but they responded to this divine blessing only by a multiplication of the external vehicles of religious devotion ('altars' and 'pillars') and disloyalty ('Their heart is false'). As a result they will suffer judgment, and Yahweh will show that he can dispense with the religious structures built supposedly to honour him. If the beginning of Israel's sin is here placed a little later in time than in 9.10, this is also the case in 10.9-10, which refers to 'the days of Gibeah' (cf. 9.9). This appears to be an allusion to the story told in Judges 19–21 about the sexual abuse of a woman visitor to the city of Gibeah. Just as in those days the other tribes had responded by waging war on the tribe of Benjamin in whose territory Gibeah was situated, so the national sin which has continued from that day will now be punished by an invasion from outside. A similar point is made in 11.1-7, 12.2-9, 13.1-3, 4-11.

But 11.1-7 leads into a remarkable passage which deserves closer attention. First it should be noted that the historical retrospect here is both longer and more emotive than in the other passages we have examined. Israel is called Yahweh's son (v. 1); and the imagery of vv. 3-4 underlines the parental nature of the relationship between God and people. It has been usual to speak of God's 'fatherly' love here, but recently it has been pointed out that the imagery is at least as appropriate to a mother's care as a father's (cf. Isa. 49.15). A second feature worthy of comment is that this passage (like 12.9 and 13.4) takes up the deliverance from Egypt at the exodus as the great sign of Yahweh's favour to his people at the beginning of their history. And yet Israel turned away from him to Baal (vv. 2-3) and refused to come back (vv. 5, 7), with exile and destruction as the result (vv. 5-6).

It is from this gloomy but apparently well-deserved prospect that we read on to verses which can properly be described as the 'pivot' of the whole book and in a sense of the whole of classical Old Testament prophecy:

> How can I give you up, Ephraim?
> > How can I hand you over, O Israel?
> How can I treat you like Admah?
> > How can I treat you like Zeboiim?
> My heart recoils within me;
> > my compassion grows warm and tender.
> I will not execute my fierce anger;
> > I will not again destroy Ephraim;
> for I am God and no mortal,
> > the Holy One in your midst,
> > and I will not come in wrath (11.8-9).

The fourfold 'How can I...?' with which these verses begin is a measure of an unresolved tension within the first seven verses of the chapter. On the one hand, here more tenderly than anywhere else, Hosea has portrayed God's care for his people which made their rejection of him so culpable; on the other, that very culpability causes him to declare, as before, their impending destruction. They have to suffer for their wrongdoing just as in the classic case of Sodom, Gomorrah and the other cities mentioned in Genesis 19. Up to this point Yahweh has been quite prepared for his love for his people to cease, for his compassion to be turned into wrath (cf. 9.15, 13.14). All his efforts to win them back to him have come to nothing. The justification for judgment is as complete as it could be. And yet Israel is his son, whom he has loved. And though an earthly father could, according to the law, in certain circumstances quite properly surrender his son to the death penalty (Deut. 21.18-21), Yahweh cannot bring himself to do this. Using language that is bold both in its anthropomorphism and in its theology, the prophet says literally that Yahweh's heart 'is turned'. Since in Hebrew the heart is the locus of purpose and will rather than of emotion, this is tantamount to saying that he has changed his mind. And we see that it is precisely this that is involved if we compare v. 9 with statements like 8.5 and 13.14. Verses 10-11 go on to speak of a return from exile (which presupposes that an exile is still to occur) and 14.4-8 more profoundly speaks of an inward moral change in Israel which will precede a renewal of their prosperity and beauty pictured in very materialistic imagery.

A Developing Message

Chapter 11, then, shows that Hosea's understanding of Yahweh's response to his people's persistent rebellion could change, and there are some further indications of this elsewhere in chs. 4–14, which we must identify before we turn back to chs. 1–3. We may begin by noting that there are some other places where Yahweh's reluctance to punish his people is mentioned.

> When I would restore the fortunes of my people,
> when I would heal Israel,
> the corruption of Ephraim is revealed... (6.11–7.1).

> I would redeem them,
> but they speak lies against me (7.13).

There are also passages where Yahweh or the prophet calls on the nation to repent and so regain divine favour, apparently in most cases in the aftermath of a national disaster (5.15; 6.1-3; 10.12; 14.1-3) but also apart from such a setting (2.6). On the other hand elsewhere the refusal, and indeed the inability, of the people to repent are mentioned as a reason for judgment or as a fault needing a cure (4.16; 5.4; 7.10; 9.17; 11.5, 7; 14.4). The temporal sequence of these different patterns of prophetic teaching is difficult to specify. But the following sequence has much to be said for it (for the detailed arguments the commentaries must be consulted):

1. Hosea seems to imply in 12.6 that the true teaching of the Israelite shrines (specifically of Bethel) is that the people should return to Yahweh and practice 'love and justice' (compare this with the much later 11.2). Further evidence that such a 'cultic call to repentance' was made at the northern shrines can perhaps be found in Ps. 81.10-16 (see further below, pp. 75-76). The complaints about Israel's stubbornness in other early oracles like 4.16 and 5.4 may be based on the fact that this teaching was being ignored, if it was heard any more at all. As a result Hosea proclaims a message of coming doom.

2. In the context of the Syro-Ephraimite war (734–731), which left much of Israel devastated by the Assyrian invaders and began to show what judgment could be like (5.11), Hosea came to see that such judgment could have a corrective purpose, to bring the people to acknowledge their guilt and return to their God (5.15). The same idea may be implicit in the words used for 'punish' and 'discipline' in 5.2 and 7.12 (*musar, yisser*), which have the connotation of correction and instruction rather than retribution. Although he seems to have believed that the political leaders' response to the disaster would bring yet more disaster (5.13-14; cf. 7.11-12, 8.9-10, etc.), he may already at this time have begun to call for the return to Yahweh which would bring a real revival of national life (one possibility is that 6.1-3 and 14.1-3 were originally spoken at this time).

3. If so, his message was still not heeded (7.10; 9.17; 11.5, 7) and most of his oracles from the 720s reverted to the uncompromising message of doom which he had

proclaimed earlier. Only, it seems, when nearly all was
lost did he break through to the insight into Yahweh's
inextinguishable love which we encounter in 11.8-11
and 14.4-8.

4. When Samaria fell in 722/21 Hosea or his disciples
may have addressed the survivors of the catastrophe
with the calls to repentance preserved in 6.1-3 and
14.1-3.

The teaching, or rather teachings, of the material in chs. 1–3
may now be considered. It is at once clear, as we have already
noted, that these chapters are held together by a combination
of sexual imagery and accounts of Hosea's relationships with
one or more women. The possible biographical implications of
the latter will be considered in a later chapter: here we are
concerned only with those prophetic sayings which refer to
and apparently provide the reason for his curious behaviour.
Within the complex structure of these chapters three main
subsections can be distinguished:

a. 1.2–2.1. A narrative in which the prophet acts and
names his children according to instructions from
Yahweh, followed by an appendix in which, without
further introductory formulae, the doom-laden significance of the children's names is reversed (1.10–2.1).

b. 2.2–23. A series of prophetic sayings of various kinds
and varied content, which with two exceptions (one
only partial) all develop the imagery of Israel as
Yahweh's wife. The exceptions are vv. 18 and 21-23
(note that in v. 22 the Hebrew reads 'I will sow *her*', so
that a link is established with the dominant metaphor
of the chapter): in vv. 21-23 the names given to the
children in ch. 1 are again reversed.

c. 3.1-5. A narrative in which the prophet again acts in
obedience to a divine command, and then explains his
action as a symbol of Yahweh's future plan for his
people.

The teaching of (a), which purports (1.2) to be from the very
beginning of Hosea's prophetic ministry, can be simply summarized. It in fact corresponds, in narrative form, to the two-

part structure which is typical of the prophetic judgment-speech against the nation (on this see below, Chapter 7, p. 97). Hosea's union with Gomer (1.2-3) is a vehicle for a condemnation of the people for their 'whoredom', their abandonment of Yahweh ('accusation'). The names given to the three children expound the consequences of this in different ways: Israel's royal house will be deposed and the nation will suffer military defeat (1.4-5); Israel will no longer be 'pitied', or loved, by Yahweh (1.6: an addition in v. 7 asserts that this does not apply to the southern kingdom of Judah); and Israel is no longer Yahweh's people nor he their God (1.8). This completes a 'threat' or 'proclamation of judgment'. An appendix (1.11) looks forward to a time when Judah and Israel (in that order, just as in the listing of the kings in 1.1) will once more experience the fulfilment of the traditional promises to the patriarchs and the exodus generation. There are good reasons (for details see the commentaries) for thinking that this appendix (like 1.7) is the work of Judaean redactors and has no contribution to make to our understanding of Hosea's own teaching. What remains is a message which fits very well with the unqualified message of judgment which we have already encountered in chs. 4 and 5, apart from the much more selective choice of imagery here, which is of course characteristic of chs. 1–3 as a whole.

(b), as already indicated, is a much more complex passage. Although some scholars have pointed to signs of a unified literary structure—and there is certainly a common element in the description of Yahweh's relationship to Israel in terms of a marriage—quite varied teachings are present here. First of all a distinction must be made between vv. 2-3, which threaten Israel with devastation as a means of persuading them to turn away from their 'whoredom', and vv. 4-13, where Yahweh has firmly decided to impose judgment on Israel. Within the latter section it is possible to make a further distinction between vv. 6-7 (which, as commentators have pointed out, break up the natural connection between v. 5 and vv. 8-9), where the coming judgment is seen as remedial in character, and the remainder of the passage, in which the typical features of the prophetic judgment-speech appear,

with the usual emphasis on retributive punishment. On the
other hand, the verses from v. 14 on look beyond the coming
judgment to a new beginning to Yahweh's relationship with
Israel. Although this to some extent involves a repetition of
past history (vv. 14-15), the keynote is the new start that will
be made, as opposed to a repair of the existing relationship.
Hence in vv. 18-20 Yahweh uses the imagery of a betrothal,
or more precisely a wedding, to describe what the future holds
for Israel.

This sequence of different variations on the basic theme
expressed in the imagery of marriage and unfaithfulness can
be closely correlated with the outline of the development of
Hosea's teaching which we have already extrapolated from
chs. 4-14. The main stock of 2.4-13 (excluding vv. 6-7)
displays the same uncompromising message of judgment
which we have encountered throughout most of chs. 4-14
(and also in the original nucleus of ch. 1). Verses 6-7 themselves correspond to the understanding of the Assyrian invasions of 734-731 as an opportunity for Israel to avoid further
judgment by a return to Yahweh (as we shall see, they are
also closely related to the basic teaching of ch. 3). The
promises of restoration which begin in v. 14 develop in different ways the new insights reached by Hosea in 11.8-9 and
14.4-8. The call to repentance in vv. 2-3 is reminiscent of similar calls in 6.1-3 and 14.1-3, but should probably not in fact be
regarded as contemporary with them, for two reasons. One is
that repentance is here seen as the way in which judgment
may be avoided, rather than the way to restoration after
judgment. The other is that the pronouncement of judgment
in vv. 4-5, 8-13 arises directly out of vv. 2-3 and presupposes
the use of symbolism which has been developed there. This
means that vv. 2-3 should be seen as evidence of the very
earliest preaching of Hosea, before he began to speak uncon-
ditionally of judgment. We have noted that something like this
seems to be presupposed by certain sayings in chs. 4-14 (4.16;
5.4).

Two interesting consequences follow from the above. The
first is that it is not ch. 1 but 2.2-3 which embodies Hosea's
earliest preaching. It may be, of course, that 1.2 reflects this

stage also, since it is concerned only with identifying Israel's sin, not with the question how or when Yahweh intends to respond to it. Secondly, it appears that, far from having been composed by Hosea at a single moment in his ministry, ch. 2 was built up by him over the years as his message developed, expressing in terms of the powerful marriage metaphor what he now understood Yahweh's total word to be. This is interesting in itself for the insight which it gives into Hosea's own handling of the problem of change and continuity in prophetic teaching, but it may also suggest that it was this growing corpus which formed both the nucleus for chs. 1–3 and the stimulus for the placing of these chapters at the beginning of the collection of Hosea's sayings.

(c) contains accounts of two connected acts of prophetic symbolism and their explanations. Again for our present purpose it is sufficient to note the teaching embodied in the explanations, leaving biographical questions for a later chapter. The significance of the first symbolic action (3.1-2) is simple but far-reaching: that despite Israel's apostasy and waywardness Yahweh (still) loves them. This is not stated in so many words, but it is probably legitimate to infer that this love is about to give rise to a new initiative on Yahweh's part which will parallel Hosea's own action (whether the latter is to be seen as an emancipation from slavery or a marriage need not concern us here). The second symbolic action indicates that the reformation and reinstatement of Israel is to be the result of a period of seclusion, during which they will be separated from objects and institutions which have presumably been the cause or at least the occasion of their downfall:

> For the Israelites shall remain many days without king or prince, without sacrifice or pillar, without ephod or teraphim. Afterwards the Israelites shall return and seek the Lord their God...(3.4-5).

The general idea of reformation through discipline suggests a date for this chapter later rather than earlier in Hosea's ministry. A date during the Syro-Ephraimite War (734–731) might be possible, but the hint of an entirely new initiative on Yahweh's part brings the chapter closer to passages like 2.14-15 and 11.8-9 which seem likely to come from a decade or so later. This is also suggested by the list of objects and institutions in v. 4, which is most completely paralleled in later oracles of Hosea. 'Sacrifice' is already mentioned in 4.13 and 4.19 and the 'ephod' and the 'teraphim' may be included among the idols mentioned in 4.12 and 4.17. But the 'pillar' or standing stone (*massebah*) is only mentioned in 10.1-2, and the removal of kings and princes only in 7.16, 8.10 (where 'cease' is probably to be read in place of NRSV's 'writhe'), 10.3, 10.7, 13.10-11. At the same time the teaching of this chapter is sufficiently distinct from the other passages which speak of a restoration for a precise dating to be impossible. Even so, it does seem from a comparison with other parts of the book that the common assumption (for that is all it is) that ch. 3 relates to an episode early in Hosea's ministry is unfounded.

To sum up, Hosea's earliest preaching would seem to be embodied in the call to repentance in 2.2-3 and perhaps in 1.2. When it was ignored, he began to proclaim a message of certain judgment which was symbolized in the names which he gave his children (1.4-9), and this continued to be his main theme throughout his ministry (2.4-5, 8-13; 4–14 *passim*). His criticisms embraced social disintegration, the failings of the political and religious leaders, corruption, and above all the worship of alien gods and the associated domination of religion by sacrifice, idolatry and other rituals. Beginning apparently from the Syro-Ephraimite War, when his earlier declarations had already been largely fulfilled, he came to look for a reforming of Israel through their suffering so that they would return to Yahweh (2.6-7; 5.15; possibly 6.1-3), but apparently this was of no avail (7.10; 11.5,7) and in the 720s he continued to proclaim doom and exile, particularly as the consequence of the politicians' foolish attempts to secure Israel's existence by diplomacy and military means alone. Reflection on Israel's historical traditions, particularly that of the exodus, eventually led him to the view that Yahweh's enduring love made it impossible for him to leave his people to their fate (3.1-2; 11.1-9) and in a series of passages he set out the form which he believed their ultimate restoration would take. This would involve a return from exile (11.11), perhaps seen as a new exodus (2.14-15), which would lead to the beginning of a new and more successful relationship between Yahweh and Israel in which Israel would respond to their God as he expected (2.16-17, 19-20; 14.4), and also to a harmonious and fruitful relationship with the natural world (2.18, 21-23; 14.5-8). But exile and the dissolution of the state would also have their part to play in this education of Israel and their return to their God (3.3-5; 14.1-3).

Further Reading

Other accounts of Hosea's teaching may be found in:

N.H. Snaith, *Mercy and Sacrifice* (London: SCM Press, 1953).

G. von Rad, *Old Testament Theology*, II (Edinburgh: Oliver & Boyd, 1965), pp. 138-46 (= *The Message of the Prophets* [London: SCM Press, 1968], pp. 110-17).

W. Brueggemann, *Tradition for Crisis* (Atlanta: John Knox, 1968).

R.E. Clements, 'Understanding the Book of Hosea', *Review and Expositor* 72 (1975), pp. 405-23.

D.R. Daniels, *Hosea and Salvation History* (BZAW, 191; Berlin: de Gruyter, 1990). This has a useful discussion of 'knowledge of God' on pp. 111-16.

On the references to 'covenant' in 6.7 and 8.2 see:

J. Day, 'Pre-Deuteronomic Allusions to the Covenant in Hosea and Psalm lxxviii', *VT* 36 (1986), pp. 1-12.

E.W. Nicholson, *God and his People* (Oxford: Clarendon Press, 1986), pp. 179-88.

Much of what is said in this chapter rests on detailed exegesis of the difficult Hebrew text of Hosea, and a commentary should be consulted for further information: see the list on pp. 11-12.

3

THE RELIGIOUS SITUATION
IN HOSEA'S TIME

NO LESS IMPORTANT than the political background for understanding what is at issue in the book of Hosea is the condition of national religion in the northern kingdom which the prophet confronted. To clarify this we need to look at statements within the book itself, which remains our most detailed source of information, but also at other evidence, some of which has come to light quite recently, which can amplify and even correct the impression which we should gain from Hosea's sayings taken alone.

A reading of the first three chapters of the book seems to suggest that in Hosea's time Israel had abandoned the worship of Yahweh for that of Baal. The situation is described mainly in metaphorical terms which portray Israel as an unfaithful wife who has turned to prostitution, with Yahweh as the deserted husband and other gods, specifically Baal, as the new recipients of Israel's favours and love (1.2; 2.5-12; 3.1). 2.13 indicates how this change of allegiance found concrete expression in acts of worship:

> the festival days of the Baals,
> when she offered incense to them
> and decked herself with her ring and jewelry,
> and went after her lovers, and forgot me,
> says the Lord.

Yet this is by no means the whole picture, as statements later in the book make clear. There, while references to Israel as 'prostituting' herself in her religious behaviour and specifically in devotion to Baal continue to appear (e.g. 4.10-12; 9.10;

11.2; 13.1), the emphasis now lies much more on a criticism of particular religious practices; and there are frequent explicit indications that Yahweh continues to be the main, if not the only, recipient of worship. Thus in 5.6 the prophet speaks about a pilgrimage to offer sacrificial worship to Yahweh which will be in vain:

> With their flocks and herds they shall go to seek the Lord,
> but they will not find him;
> he has withdrawn from them.

In 8.2 Yahweh quotes a cry of supplication:

> Israel cries to me,
> 'My God, we—Israel—know you!'

The references to 'the house of the Lord' (cf. 8.1; 9.4) probably also presuppose that temples dedicated to Yahweh continued to be in regular use.

The difference between chs. 1–3 and chs. 4ff. was a major reason for Y. Kaufman's view, also maintained by H.L. Ginsberg, that these two collections of sayings come from two different prophets, one living in the mid-ninth century (under Ahab when Baal-worship was rife) and the other in the eighth century (when the issue was the corruption of Yahwism itself). That view is certainly to be rejected, both because it requires unsupported emendations to the text of ch. 1 and because it ignores the extent to which the themes of chs. 1–3 continue to appear, albeit less prominently, in chs. 4–14 (see above). But the evidence of these latter chapters does require a more nuanced view of the religious situation in Hosea's time than one which sees it as characterized by wholesale abandonment of Yahweh for Baal. For example it is possible to suppose that the worship of Yahweh had been so corrupted by elements of a Canaanite origin that, although Yahweh was worshipped in name, in practice it was as if he had been replaced by Baal. That some 'Baalization' of Yahweh-worship had taken place is probably indicated explicitly in 2.16: 'On that day, says the Lord, you will call me, "My husband", and no longer will you call me, "My Baal".' The use of the title 'Baal' (for that is what it is) as an epithet for Yahweh could in theory be harmless enough, since it can

mean simply 'lord' or 'husband', but in a religious context its
associations with the Canaanite storm-god Baal-Hadad would
almost certainly have affected the way in which Yahweh was
thought of and worshipped. However, while this theory may
well be an accurate understanding of one aspect of the
religious situation, it probably does not do sufficient justice to
everything that Hosea says, particularly in chs. 1–3. The
references to Israel's 'lovers' in the plural and to 'the days of
the Baals' (2.13), as well as the whole imagery of prostitution,
are most naturally taken to refer to an explicit offering of
worship to Baal and 'other gods' (3.1). This may indeed have
included the worship of a goddess. At the end of ch. 4 the
Hebrew text includes some feminine pronominal suffixes
which modern English translations may too quickly have
emended away (contrast AV). Verses 18-19 should probably be
translated:

> When their drinking is ended, they indulge in sexual orgies;
>   they are infatuated with her whose shameless devotees
>   are a disgrace.
> A wind has wrapped her in her skirts,
>   and they shall be ashamed because of their altars.

The 'her' would be a goddess (probably Asherah or Astarte)
whom Hosea hesitates to name. There are also two obscure
passages which may refer to a 'High One' (ʿal) as the object of
Israel's misplaced devotion (7.16 [NRSV 'that which does not
profit' is based on an emendation]; 11.7). It seems necessary,
therefore, to envisage a situation in which Yahweh, Baal and
probably some other deity or deities were worshipped side by
side. Only such a picture will do justice to all the evidence. On
the basis of ch. 2 it is perhaps possible to go a little further,
since there the worship of Baal is quite specifically linked with
a particular aspect of religion and everyday life, namely the
securing of a good harvest from the land. As will be seen
below, this is precisely the need which Baal was thought to
meet in Canaanite religion. 9.1 points in the same direction, as
the reference here is clearly to celebrations at the harvest,
and it is significant that it is in this context that the prophet
warns his hearers against conforming to the practices of 'other
nations'. The evidence thus points to a situation in which Baal

was worshipped in festivals concerned with the harvest, while
Yahweh continued to be the national god in other respects, for
example in war.

The book of Hosea, particularly chs. 4–14, often refers to
contemporary religious practices, many of which the prophet
regarded as quite improper, even though they were not necessarily associated with the worship of a deity other than
Yahweh. These include divination (3.4; 4.12), hilltop shrines
under trees (4.13), temple prostitution (4.14), the making of
idols (4.17; 8.4; 11.2; 13.2; 14.3, 8), wailing and self-mutilation
(7.14), golden calf/calves (8.5-6; 10.5-6; 13.2), and the multiplication of pillars (*maṣṣebot*) (3.4; 10.1). Altars, sacrifices and
festivals are constantly on Hosea's lips (2.11, 13; 3.4; 4.13-14;
4.19; 5.6; 6.6; 8.11, 13; 9.4-5; 10.1, 8; 11.2; 12.11; 13.2) as are
priests (4.4-6; 5.1; 6.9; 10.5), and specific criticism is made of
shrines at Bethel/Beth-aven (4.15; 6.10 [read 'Bethel' for 'the
house of Israel']; 10.5, 8, 15; 12.4), Gilgal (4.15; 9.15; 12.11)
and probably Mizpah, Tabor and Shittim (5.1-2).

Archaeological Evidence

Clarification of some of the religious phenomena mentioned
above is available from a number of sources. The situation has
much in common with that which is represented in the stories
of Elijah a century earlier (especially 1 Kgs 18; 2 Kgs 1),
when the Omride dynasty's alliance with Phoenicia had led to
official royal support for pagan worship (1 Kgs 16.31-33). But
this had come to an end, according to 2 Kings 9–10, with the
revolution of Jehu. Presumably since then the worship of Baal
had been revived in circumstances that are no longer clear, or
perhaps, at least at a popular level, it had never fully ceased.
The golden calves went back to the original cult reforms of
Jeroboam I at the beginning of the independent northern
kingdom (1 Kgs 12.27-33): their religious character and
associations will be discussed below. Many of the practices
which Hosea condemns were understood at an earlier stage of
scholarship purely in the context of the magic and nature-
religion which was then thought to be characteristic of
Canaanite religion, and the Baals were thought of as local

numina, the divine 'lords' each of a particular piece of territory. The modern understanding of Canaanite religion, however, has been transformed by the discovery since 1929 of the
mythological texts from the fourteenth century BCE at Ras
Shamra, ancient Ugarit, on the Syrian coast, and it is now
possible to give a much fuller picture of the religious beliefs
which, subtly or more openly, were challenging the traditions
of Yahwism in Hosea's time. A brief account of some other
archaeological discoveries is also appropriate here.

The most important texts from Ugarit for our purpose are
those which have been entitled by modern scholars 'Baal and
Yam', 'The Palace of Baal' and 'Baal and Mot' (see *ANET*,
pp. 129-41; they correspond to nos. 1-9 in the newer numbering
system used by J.C.L. Gibson). These are stories about the
gods of the Ugaritic pantheon, over whom the God Ilu (El)
and his consort Athirat (Asherah) presided, but as the titles of
the stories imply Baal is the leading character in all three
texts. 'Baal and Yam' recounts a struggle over kingship among
the gods. El has decided to elevate his son Yam, the god of the
sea, to be king over the other gods and he commands the
craftsman-god Kothar-wa-Khasis to build him a palace. Baal
(who according to one version of the story had previously
been king of the gods) challenges Yam and eventually, after
initial setbacks which require him to obtain new weapons,
succeeds in conquering and killing him.

'The Palace of Baal' is probably the sequel to this. Baal, who
as the storm-god alone knows the secret of the lightning,
bemoans his lack of a palace and obtains the help of the goddesses Anat and Athirat in persuading El to let him have one.
A palace of silver and gold is built for him and, after a ban-
quet to celebrate its completion, Baal is persuaded to have a
window opened in the palace, which is said to correspond to a
'rift' in the clouds. Through this he 'utters his holy voice' (the
thunder), which makes the earth and its inhabitants tremble,
and he invites Mot (the god of death) to devour any who
challenge his rule. In the third text Mot again appears, but
this time as Baal's enemy. Mot summons Baal to the under-
world, and Baal seems compelled to agree, though he endeav-
ours unsuccessfully by a subterfuge to pass off the offspring

of his intercourse with a cow as a substitute for himself. On hearing of Baal's 'death' the other gods lacerate themselves in mourning. Subsequently he is released from Mot's power by his sister Anat's intervention, which promises renewed fertility, and after a trial of strength Mot finally acknowledges that Baal is supreme.

In the first place, these myths enable us to realize very vividly the extent of the difference between the Canaanite conception of the gods and the kind of theology which predominates in the Old Testament, even if traces of polytheism can still be detected in some biblical passages (e.g. Ps. 29; 48.2; 74.13-17; 93). In these myths the gods are subject to very human limitations and foibles, their decisions depend not so much on purposeful plans as on tricks and fights, and human beings appear only in the background. Yet the modern study of myth has made it clear that these stories are concerned with very central issues in the life of an ancient society. The struggle for kingship in 'Baal and Yam', as in similar stories elsewhere in the ancient Near East, affirms Baal's control over forces of chaos which might threaten his rule and the stability of the cosmos. Baal's palace is the heavenly counterpart of his earthly temple and the story demonstrates how the fulfilment of his life-giving role in the provision of rain is dependent upon the existence of a temple where he can 'dwell' and be worshipped. In 'Baal and Mot' there is a recognition of the alternating sequence of rain and drought in the Mediterranean climate, which must have led to the fear that the storm-god had himself succumbed to the all-embracing power of death: but worshippers are reassured that he has not gone for ever, and a rationale is provided for some of their ritual practices.

It cannot be assumed that precisely these myths were in circulation in Hosea's day—the surviving texts are from 600 years before his time and Ugarit lay 250 miles north of Samaria—but even so they probably provide us with the best indication that we can have of the kind of thinking that was expressed in the worship of Baal. Other texts from Ugarit give details of the prominent part played by sacrifice in the religious life of the city, including the rituals at the temple of

Baal. From Canaan itself textual evidence of this kind is practically non-existent (though the Amarna letters contain a few expressions of religious belief), but archaeological excavations have uncovered numerous examples of shrines from both the Canaanite and Israelite periods which illustrate the objects and practices to which Hosea refers in a general way.

For example, Late Bronze Age temples at Hazor (Area C) and Shechem contained pillars (*maṣṣebot*), in one instance inside and in the other at the entrance to the building, and an Israelite sanctuary in the fortress at Arad (dating from the monarchy period) had *maṣṣebot* in its inner cult-room. These may have served to symbolize the active presence of the deity. At all these sites there were also altars in the courtyards of temples for animal sacrifices (at Hazor in Area H). A recent discovery from the period of the Judges has shown how early in Israel's history images of bulls (or 'calves', as Hosea calls them) were associated with worship. In the excavation of a hill-top site between Nablus and Jenin a bronze figurine of a young bull was discovered, with what may be a *maṣṣebah* and an incense-burner. In fact the bull has a long history as a religious symbol in Canaan. It appears sometimes to represent a kind of pedestal on which a god was portrayed as standing, but elsewhere to symbolize the power of the divine presence itself. In the Ugaritic myths El is frequently referred to as 'the bull', and the title 'Mighty One', applied to Yahweh in the Old Testament, is so similar to a word for 'bull' that some scholars believe that this was its original connotation. There has been much argument over whether the golden calves set up by Jeroboam I and referred to by Hosea (8.5-6; 10.5-6; 13.2) were really images of Yahweh or originally just pedestals upon which he was thought to be invisibly present. The statements in the Old Testament certainly favour the former alternative, though it must be recognized that they all occur in texts whose authors were very critical of these religious objects and who may have exaggerated the significance which was originally attached to them. In any case it is clear even from the polemical account in 1 Kings 12 that golden calves were associated with the worship of Yahweh as the God of the exodus (compare also Exod. 32.4), and there is no justification for seeing them as images of Baal.

Most of the evidence surveyed, important as it is, is of only general relevance for understanding the religious situation which Hosea confronted. But some archaeological discoveries have been made which, from their much closer proximity in space and time, offer a more direct indication of contemporary beliefs and practices. In the excavations at Samaria, the capital of the northern kingdom from early in the ninth century BCE, inscribed potsherds (ostraca) were found which record deliveries of wine and oil to the royal palace. These appear to date from the first half of the eighth century, only shortly before Hosea's prophetic activity. They include a large number of personal names, many of which incorporate a shortened form of the name Yahweh, Yaw. But some are formed with the divine name Baal, such as Abibaal, Baalazkar, Baala (an abbreviated name) and Meribaal—a clear indication of a readiness in the circles from which these ostraca derive to recognize the power of Baal as well as of Yahweh. Not all these names include a divine element, but of those that do there are eight which include the element 'Baal' over against eleven which include 'Yaw', a surprisingly high ratio. Further evidence of the worship of Baal appears in the inscriptions from Kuntillet 'Ajrud. Although this site is located far to the south, between Gaza and Eilat, it appears that citizens of the northern kingdom were among those who visited it. This is indicated both by the fact that personal names ending in -yaw (as at Samaria) instead of -yahu (the Judaean form) occur in the inscriptions and by a reference to 'Yahweh of Samaria' in one of them. These texts, which are now dated to the early eighth century, consist mainly of blessings and prayers inscribed on the plastered walls of a building and, in certain cases, on large jars (pithoi). One of the inscriptions on plaster appears to read:

When [...] El appeared, the mountains melted,
Blessed be Baal on the day of wa[r],
By the name of El on the day of wa[r].

This is an unusual text, perhaps part of a hymn. It is reported that the name of Baal occurs in some other texts from

Kuntillet 'Ajrud, but no details of these have been published so far. Much more common, at least in the texts that have been published, is the name Yahweh. But even where it occurs there is sometimes a sign of the Canaanite influence which is so abominable to Hosea. The following blessings occur:

> I bless you (pl.) by Yahweh of Samaria and by his asherah.
> I bless you (sing.) by Yahweh of Teman and by his asherah.

The closing phrase of each of these sentences has been understood by some scholars to mean that the blessing is in the name of the goddess Asherah as well as Yahweh, so that just as Athirat/Asherah was El's consort at Ugarit, so Asherah was Yahweh's consort in this polytheistic form of Yahwism. However, the grammatical form makes this unlikely, as a possessive suffix cannot be attached to a proper name, and it is more likely that we have here two references to a cultic symbol, '*the* asherah', which is also mentioned in several Old Testament passages as well as in another inscription from Khirbet el-Qom in Judah. This was probably a wooden pole and to judge from its name it most likely symbolized the presence and power of the goddess of the same name. It is particularly significant that according to 1 Kgs 16.33 Ahab had set up such a symbol, probably in Samaria, which was apparently still there in the late ninth century (2 Kgs 13.6). There is no record in the Old Testament of its removal, and it may well have remained in place until the destruction of the city by the Assyrians in 722. Strangely Hosea does not mention it explicitly, though the goddess alluded to in 4.18-19 could be Asherah, and the 'idols' which he mentions several times (e.g. 4.17) would presumably have included the small clay figurines of a naked goddess of which so many examples have been found in excavations.

One final recent archaeological discovery should be mentioned here. In 1967 a Dutch expedition excavating at Tell Deir 'Alla in the Jordan Valley near its confluence with the Jabbok came upon numerous fragments of inscribed plaster which, when they had been reassembled as far as was possible, proved to contain a text or texts about the seer Balaam the son of Beor. However, in contrast with the story about him in the Bible (Num. 22–24), he here appears not as the mouthpiece of Yahweh but as speaking after a vision of 'the gods' who seem to be led by a goddess named Sheger and a god Ashtar who is known from other texts. The script of the text has been variously dated, but both palaeography and the archaeological context are now thought to favour an origin for the inscription about 750 BCE. Its language has been the subject of much debate: it seems not to be Hebrew, but some regard it as Aramaic and others as a dialect which is best described as 'Gileadite'.

Geographically Tell Deir 'Alla seems to have fallen within Israelite territory, at least in the mid-eighth century, for Jeroboam II had apparently succeeded in recapturing the Israelite lands in Transjordan from Syria (2 Kgs 14.25; see 10.32-33 for their loss a century or so earlier). Hosea refers to Gilead as Israelite in 6.8 and 12.11. No doubt the religion of the inhabitants of Tell Deir 'Alla had been affected by the period of foreign rule, but they may have been not untypical of the whole region of Gilead in this. From the little we know it seems likely that Sheger and Ashtar were thought to be responsible for the fertility of the flocks and herds: the words *sheger* and *'ashtarot* occur together with reference to young animals in Deut. 7.13. So in this respect the Balaam text would confirm the same sort of drift into paganism for the sake of fertility as we saw attested in Hosea chs. 2 and 9.

Popular and Court Religion

H. Balz-Cochois has sought to reconstruct more fully and more sympathetically the character of the popular religious beliefs and practices which Hosea condemned. She lays most stress on the practices described in Hosea 4, so that her research takes a rather different direction from reconstructions like ours which have focused largely on the information to be derived from the Ugaritic texts. This is not necessarily a bad thing, because the mythological texts come essentially from a literate class (though it seems that they were also recited for the benefit of those who could not read), and the popular religion, especially in rural areas, may have been rather different. Certainly it is with rural shrines that Hosea seems to be concerned in 4.12-14. The difference may be one of emphasis rather than a complete opposition—the myths themselves seem in places to presuppose rituals like those attested in Hosea 4—but it is a useful corrective to have some attention focused once again on the rituals themselves and their significance, and if Balz-Cochois is even approximately right in her interpretation there was a much stronger 'female' element in them than is suggested by an exclusive concentration on the myths about Baal.

Ironically the fullest direct information about this rural religion comes from the Old Testament texts themselves. According to Balz-Cochois it had three main elements: devotion to the Baalim (cf. Hos. 2.13, 17; 11.2) whom she takes to be local *numina*, not necessarily manifestations of the cosmic Baal; communication with spirits and the dead (cf. the *teraphim* in Hos. 3.4 and probably 4.12); and the prominence of female deities, especially Asherah the earth-mother goddess and Astarte 'the erotic-aggressive goddess'. As we have seen, explicit references to these goddesses are rare, if present at all, in Hosea. Balz-Cochois shows that the idea of Baal's fertilizing the earth (conceived as a mother-goddess) is based on much later texts and should not be seen as the key to the polemic in Hos. 1.2. However, better evidence of devotion to goddesses is to be found in the probability that the 'sacred groves' of 4.13 were dedicated to Asherah and that cultic prostitution (4.14) involved the dedication of the sex-drive to Astarte (not, in Balz-Cochois' view, the securing of fertility by sympathetic magic). Influence from the Astarte-cult is detected in Hos. 2.14-15 and, more plausibly, from the Asherah-cult in Hos. 2.18-23 and 14.9.

In attempting to describe the sexual rituals of the rural high places Balz-Cochois distinguishes three separate practices. First, she accepts the theory that ordinary young women in Israel, as among other Near Eastern peoples, dedicated their sexuality to the gods before marriage by intercourse at the shrines. As propounded in Wolff's commentary on Hosea this theory affirmed that *all* young Israelite women in Hosea's time were required to submit to such a ritual, but W. Rudolph showed that a universal practice of this kind could not be proved and was contradicted by some Old Testament evidence. He allowed, nevertheless, that some young Israelite women might have taken part in such ritual intercourse and it is in this form (with rather more confidence than Rudolph) that Balz-Cochois presents the theory as an explanation of what is described in Hos. 4.13-14a. In her opinion the sexual drive of these young women was dedicated to Astarte and Asherah, not to Baal as Wolff had thought. Secondly, there was so-called sacred prostitution, which is referred to in Hos. 4.14b and which clearly involved female members of the cult personnel in what Balz-Cochois sees as acts of dedication of their sexual desires to Astarte in partnership with priests or, possibly, with other male members of the community. Thirdly, a general freedom of sexual intercourse may have existed at the festivals, in which ordinary prostitutes ('whores' in 4.14) and married women would take part (cf. the references to 'adultery' in 4.14 and 'illegitimate children' in 5.7). Balz-Cochois suggests that sex thus became a matter of communal enjoyment with a religious dimension in much the same way as was the eating of the meat of a sacrificial animal. Common to all these rites were what she calls 'realism' and ecstasy. By 'realism' she means an acknowledgment that basic human needs have to be satisfied, whether for food or for sex; and that if Yahwism did not appear to provide for their satisfaction there were other rituals that could.

Some features of Balz-Cochois' vivid account (of which only a part has been summarized here) are certainly over-adventurous. There is not a little speculation involved in it, and some popular practices are included which though known from elsewhere in the Old Testament are not mentioned by Hosea (that need not of course mean that they did not exist among his contemporaries). A more serious criticism is that she tends to prefer a cultic interpretation where a more general one may be appropriate. It is, for example, possible to read 4.13b-14a in entirely non-cultic terms, as a reference to the promiscuity in everyday life of younger women, which the older men are all too ready to condemn despite their own involvement in extramarital sexual behaviour at the shrines (so Rudolph and some other commentators). Nevertheless, even if the picture of the rural religion of Hosea's times is in some respects overdrawn, and in others even inaccurate (e.g. there is no particular reason to see the priest of 4.4-6 as an officiant at one of the hill-top shrines), the attempt to understand it in its own terms is a worthwhile one and rightly draws attention to the probable involvement of goddesses in this popular cult. We have seen above that some recent archaeological discoveries, apparently unknown to Balz-Cochois, have confirmed the importance of this precisely in Hosea's time.

Another recent study of the background to Hosea's religious polemic has given prominence to a very different aspect of it: the close connection between some religious practices and objects and the monarchy. Much has been written about 'sacral kingship' and the role of the Davidic kings in the temple cult of Jerusalem, but accounts of the religious role of the northern kings have tended to limit themselves to repeating the very polemical reports presented in the books of Kings. H. Utzschneider has noted, however, that in several passages Hosea's criticism of the northern kings is closely connected with reference to the cult, in a way that suggests that the cult may have played a role in legitimating the monarchy, as it apparently did in the southern kingdom (see especially Ps. 2 and 110). The passages in question are Hos. 8.4, 10.3 and 13.11, all of which occur in close connection with references to the golden calf/calves and other aspects of worship (8.5; 10.5; 13.2). It is of course with Hosea's association of these themes that we are dealing in these passages (or even perhaps an association created by his disciples or editors), and Utzschneider's main contention is that according to Hosea the kings are disqualified from office by their encouragement of what he saw as unwanted or illicit religious practices. But the association probably had deeper roots then this. The regular association of the king and the ruling elite with the cult (cf. also 5.1; 8.10-14; 9.15; 10.7-8, 15) would have much greater significance if it was based on the belief that the worship of Yahweh which centred on the calf-images could be relied upon to sustain the monarchy in times of danger and uncertainty. Just such a confidence is probably implied in the reference to

Bethel as 'the king's sanctuary' in Amos 7.14 and in the congregational prayer for a king in Ps. 80.17, which there are strong reasons for associating with the northern kingdom in its closing years.

Further Reading

The view that chs. 1–3 and 4–14 of the book of Hosea come from different prophets who lived a century apart is presented by two Jewish scholars:

Y. Kaufmann, *The Religion of Israel* (abridged edn; London: Allen & Unwin, 1961), pp. 368-77.

H.L. Ginsberg, 'Hosea, Book of', in *EncJud*, VIII, cols. 1010-1025.

A clear account of the mythological texts and other discoveries at Ugarit is given in:

A.H.W. Curtis, *Ugarit* (Cities of the Biblical World; Cambridge: Lutterworth Press, 1985).

The major texts can be found, with introductions and translations, in:

J.C.L. Gibson, *Canaanite Myths and Legends* (Edinburgh: T. & T. Clark, 2nd edn, 1978).

On the discoveries in Palestine itself mentioned in this chapter see:

P.J. King, *Amos, Hosea and Micah: An Archaeological Commentary* (Philadelphia: Westminster Press, 1988), pp. 88-107.

K.A.D. Smelik, *Ancient Hebrew Writings* (Edinburgh: T. & T. Clark, 1991), pp. 150-67.

The two recent studies of Israelite religion mentioned in the text are both in German:

H. Balz-Cochois, *Gomer. Der Höhenkult Israels im Selbstverständnis der Volksfrömmigkeit. Untersuchungen zu Hosea 4,1—5, 7* (Europäische Hochschulschriften XXIII/191; Frankfurt and Berne: Lang, 1982).

H. Utzschneider, *Hosea: Prophet vor dem Ende* (OBO, 31; Freiburg: Universitätsverlag and Göttingen: Vandenhoeck & Ruprecht, 1980).

4

HOSEA AND
ISRAELITE SOCIETY

IN RECENT YEARS Old Testament scholars have shown an increasing interest in the social sciences, and the study of the prophets is no exception (see the studies by A.D.H. Mayes and R.P. Carroll listed at the end of the chapter for a fuller account than can be given here). Indeed Old Testament prophecy has long attracted considerable interest from sociologists such as Max Weber and Peter Berger, whose aim has been to identify in very general terms the typical features of human social organization. Such work promises to shed new light on Hosea's background, his prophetic ministry and his impact on later generations. It must be acknowledged that specific studies of this kind on Hosea are as yet few and far between. Even so, much earlier study of Hosea has touched on what are in essence sociological questions, and general works on Old Testament prophecy written from a sociological perspective give some indication of topics that could be fruitfully examined in connection with Hosea, and may allow some provisional conclusions to be drawn.

Sociology is a subject with a wide range of methods and interests and as with most scholarly disciplines, it is possible to distinguish a variety of 'schools of thought' which have had a major influence on sociological research and continue to do so. As we consider the possibilities for a sociological approach to Hosea, we shall therefore need to be alive to the different issues which have been or could be raised from this perspective. Fortunately some valuable clarification has already been provided at this point by Mayes, who has made the distinction between the 'conflict tradition' of sociology inspired by Marx and Weber and the 'functionalist' tradition inspired by Durkheim into the organizing principle for his accounts of sociological research on the Old Testament. Mayes summarizes the difference as follows:

> For Weber society is a mode of organization of individuals and sociology is the study of the understandable and purposive actions of such individuals; for Durkheim society is the prior reality, and social phenomena are *sui generis* realities to be understood only in relation to other social phenomena rather than by reference to the psychology of the individual.

Of course in academic research (as in the world which it studies) things are rarely so simple: particular investigations may draw on elements from both schools of thought, and another recent writer on the history of sociology, R. Collins, has found it necessary to add a third 'tradition' to those highlighted by Mayes: 'microinteractionism', a specifically American tradition which seeks to bridge the gap between individualist and collectivist theories by introducing the notion of the individual living within a socially constructed perception of reality. Its best-known representative in theological circles is Peter Berger; some applications of it to the study of prophecy will be discussed below. These distinctions are a useful beginning to any attempt to understand the varied aspects of 'prophecy and society' which have been studied by Old Testament scholars.

One such aspect which at first sight lies on the periphery of the study of prophecy as such is the investigation of the general social changes in the period of the monarchy which have long been seen as a contributory factor to the rise of eighth-century prophecy. The oracles of Amos, Micah and Isaiah in particular bear witness to a widening gap between rich and poor, behind which a complex network of causes and effects can be discerned. The incorporation of Canaanite districts into Israel, the growth of cities, the development of a royal administrative and taxation system, foreign trade (including luxury items) and the success of large-scale enterprises in agricultural and related activities all played a part in making Israel a very different kind of society in the eighth century from what it had been in the eleventh century. Attention has properly been drawn to evidence that royal intervention was involved in each of these developments: national security and the need for the kings to reward their 'servants', not to speak of the struggles for the throne, particularly in the northern kingdom, were constant destabilizing factors. Hosea does not have as much to say about specific aspects of this situation as do the other eighth-century prophets (note, however, 4.2; 7.3-7; 12.1, 7-8)—his emphasis lies elsewhere—but he does refer to it in a deeper and more general way when he laments the breakdown in social relationships caused by the disappearance of faithfulness and loyalty (4.1: cf. 6.4, 6); and it clearly played some part in the shaping of his message.

A different kind of sociological study of prophecy is concerned with its social location. This seeks to establish the links which prophets had with the major institutions of ancient Israelite society such as the cult or the royal court. These are subjects in which Old Testament study has long been interested, without any specifically sociological impulses, but it should be noted that one view of prophecy which was very influential in the late nineteenth and early twentieth centuries so emphasized the originality of the thought of the classical prophets and their independence and isolation, as individuals, from their contemporaries that it could only find room for an investigation of such links in the case of early 'pre-classical' prophets such as we meet in the books of Samuel and Kings. Even Max Weber, who brought sociological ideas to bear on many aspects of ancient Israelite religion and society, was so strongly influenced by this scholarly tradition that he characterized the new kind of prophecy which began to emerge in the ninth century with Elijah as the product of 'a stratum of genteel intellectuals' who were opposed to the official institutions of priesthood and monarchy. Such a view (which shows some signs of re-emerging today) of course leaves room for sociological questions of kinds which we have yet to consider, but not that at present under discussion.

Many scholars from the 1930s on have in varying degrees maintained that the origins at least of the classical prophets lay much closer to the traditional institutions of Israelite religion and society than had been supposed. Particular emphasis has been placed by these scholars on the extent to which these prophets were related to and dependent upon the cultic institutions such as the temples of Judah and Israel and the major festivals celebrated at them. Such an involvement with the public worship of the people might, it has been thought, have taken a variety of forms, from a general familiarity with the themes and theology of worship at the temples to actual participation by the prophet in a formal liturgical setting. A famous essay by Peter Berger brought this development within Old Testament research to the attention of sociologists and used it to modify Weber's sharp antithesis between the notions of charisma and institution. This issue as far as it concerns Hosea will be examined more thoroughly in Chapter 5; but it may be noted here that there is wide agreement that passages like Hos. 4.4-6 and 9.1-9 make best sense on the assumption that they were spoken at a temple during the celebration of one of the great festivals.

Prophecy as an Institution

A third line of research works from the idea that prophecy itself was in some sense or senses an institution of ancient Israelite society. Earlier studies had focused particularly on the prophetic groups or coenobia which appear frequently in the historical books of the Old Testament (e.g. 1 Sam. 9; 2 Kgs 1–2) and sought to identify their distinctive lifestyles and activities. It was natural to ask what relation the classical prophets might have borne to such groups, and the early tendency was to separate them as much from their forebears, despite the use of the same title 'prophet', as from the other institutions of Israelite society. But in a somewhat similar (and indeed related) development in scholarship to that mentioned above it came to be stressed by scholars such as H.H. Rowley and R.E. Clements that the differences between the early prophets and the classical prophets were far less significant than had previously been thought. Discussion about the proper translation of Amos 7.14 has been central to this debate. In the case of Hosea it should be noted that his references to (presumably earlier) prophets are positive (6.5; 9.8; 12.10, 13; in 4.5 the threat against 'the prophet' is probably redactional, and 9.7b is a quotation of Hosea's opponent[s]), even though in 1.4 he does seem to take a very different view of Jehu's rebellion from that of Elisha. Equally, studies of Ezekiel by W. Zimmerli, of Amos and Hosea by H.W. Wolff and of Isaiah by numerous scholars greatly qualified the isolation of these prophets by arguing that the books named after them presuppose the existence of a group of 'disciples' who handed on and reinterpreted their master's teaching. Unfortunately very little is known directly about the composition and behaviour of such prophetic groups in Israel, and a good deal of what is written about them is based on inference, sometimes supported by parallels drawn with better-attested phenomena in other societies.

In recent years concepts have been employed which are derived from newer sociological and anthropological research, in an awareness that older concepts such as 'charisma' and 'office' had serious deficiencies for the study of Israelite prophecy. Thus R.R. Wilson has made extensive use of the contrast between 'central' and 'peripheral' intermediaries, a concept taken over with some adaptation from I.M. Lewis's work *Ecstatic Religion* (1971). He also explores the idea of the 'support group' which is held to be particularly important to a 'peripheral' intermediary as providing the kind of encouragement and regulation which the central institutions of a society as a whole might provide for a 'central' intermediary. According to Wilson Hosea was a peripheral prophet who challenged the central priesthood of the northern kingdom and was repudiated by them (cf. 4.4-6; 9.7-9). His support was derived from a somewhat ill-defined group ('the Ephraimite tradition of prophecy') which is also to be seen behind the Elohistic source of the Pentateuch, the Deuteronomic literature and ultimately Jeremiah. This may have originated in the priesthood at Shiloh in pre-monarchic times. There is some similarity here to the view of Morton Smith and B. Lang that Hosea belonged to a 'Yahweh-alone party' which challenged the originally polytheistic character of Israelite religion.

Wilson's summary of sociological research is useful and his effort to present a comprehensive sociological account of prophecy in Israel is a bold undertaking, but his application of sociological terms tends to be imprecise and he often does not succeed in doing more than to give new labels to features that had been recognized, or at least inferred, earlier.

D.L. Petersen's approach is both more limited and more productive. He takes up what has come to be known as 'role theory', a branch of social psychology which has also been much used by G. Theissen in his *Sociology of Early Palestinian Christianity* (1978). This seeks to define the 'parts' played by individuals in social life by describing such things as their characteristic activities, the physical and mental skills required and the expectations which others in society have of the role-player. In contrast to 'status', 'role' is a dynamic concept and has to do with observable conduct. An individual may enact more than one role and a role may involve the self to a greater or lesser extent. One particularly high level of involvement (though not the highest) is ecstasy, but Petersen concludes (for non-sociological reasons) that ecstasy is not a regular feature of Israelite prophecy: prophetic activities involve lower levels of self-involvement, particularly what theorists have referred to as 'engrossed acting'. Much of the rest of Petersen's book is concerned with the examination of the 'role-labels' *ro'eh* ('seer'), *'ish-'elohim* ('man of god'), *hozeh* ('seer') and *nabi'* ('prophet'). His conclusion is that the first of these is a living role-label only in the folk-tale embedded in 1 Samuel 9; the second corresponds closely to Lewis's 'peripheral prophets' (a term which Wilson had unjustifiably widened); while the other two terms both referred to 'central morality prophets', *hozeh* being the normal word in the south and *nabi'* in the north. These two terms are not exact synonyms, however, as they are related to differences in the conceptions of prophecy held respectively in the south and north, differences which derive from the different overall structures of Yahwism in the two kingdoms. In the north the prophet (*nabi'*) is a 'covenant spokesman', in the south he (as a *hozeh*) has received a call in the divine council and functions in the first place as a herald to the royal court rather than to the people at large. Hosea uses only the term *nabi'* (see above). It is true that in much of the Old Testament literature the terms appear to be interchangeable, but this can be attributed to the mixing of traditions, and perhaps of terms, which took place from the late eighth century onwards.

Perhaps the most interesting aspect of this subject of role-labels as far as Hosea is concerned is that there is no certain example of his applying the term *nabi'* to himself. In 9.7 it is generally agreed that like 'the man of the spirit' it is a term used of him by others; in 9.8 it may well be a later gloss. This does not mean that Hosea disapproved of the *nebi'im*: his genuine references to them (6.5, 12.10, 13) suggest the opposite. But it may suggest that he perceived his own role to be something new. His own image—it is not a formal role-description—is that of 'watchman (of Ephraim)' (9.8: cf. 8.1?), an expression which Jeremiah (6.17) and Ezekiel (3.17) later took up along with other Hosean themes. A sociological approach to prophecy as much as any other has to be alive to the radically new features of eighth-century prophecy as well as its more traditional aspects.

Finally under this heading we must introduce the work of H. Utzschneider, which is the only book-length study of Hosea from a sociological point of view to appear so far. Much of its contents more properly belongs under the next main heading (the study of the prophet's view of the social institutions of his time, and its basis), and here we shall examine only his understanding of prophecy itself as an institution. Utzschneider approaches this issue with the help of the general account of institutions given by Berger and Luckmann in their book, *The Social Construction of Reality* (1966), a book whose thesis is closely related to the 'role theory' mentioned earlier. This account takes language itself as the basic example of an institution: it is a given system of expression and communication through which the individual relates to his wider social context. On this view an institution need not mean an organized structure of human relationships like a school or a business: it exists wherever actions of a particular kind are regularly performed by agents in a particular category. This view has the advantage for the study of prophecy that it does not limit investigation to an examination only of those more obvious social structures such as the royal court and the cult, to which prophecy has sometimes but not always been related, or to the forms of association (*coenobia*) which it sometimes but not always adopts for itself. Utzschneider recognizes that the institution of prophecy is linked in a kind of network with other institutions (a general characteristic of institutions which Berger and Luckmann also note), but is primarily to be defined by its own typical activities. One final introductory point of great importance to Utzschneider is that Berger and Luckmann's concept of an institution emphasizes its historical dimension:

> Institutions always have a history of which they are the products. It is impossible to understand an institution adequately without an understanding of the historical process in which it was produced...The transmission of the meaning of an institution is based on the social recognition of that institution as a 'permanent' solution to a 'permanent' problem of the given collectivity. Therefore potential actors of institutionalized actions must be *systematically* acquainted with those meanings. This necessitates some form of 'educational' process.

In addition to the origins and the maintenance of an institution, this historical dimension also means, as Utzschneider usefully points out, the susceptibility of an institution to change as a result of historical events at particular times.

But what are the typical activities that define the institution of prophecy? Unlike many general textbooks on prophecy, which try to answer this question with reference to early Israelite prophecy, Utzschneider chooses to make his 'cross-section' in the history of the institution at the point represented by one of the classical prophets: Hosea. The key features of Hosea's prophetic activity are not easy to disentangle from Utzschneider's detailed discussion. It is clear that they include the claim to make critical comments on the institutions of the royal court and the cultic shrines, a matter with which we shall deal in a later section. Apart from this, the most relevant section of Utzschneider's book for our present purpose is that in which he examines in detail two of the passages in which references to prophets occur, 6.4-5 and 9.1-9.

Both passages are understood as pointing to a 'legal' conception of the prophetic office on Hosea's part. The former passage connects this office with the emergence of divine *mišpaṭ*,
'justice', 'the theocratic order of life', but in the sense that the
prophet is an advocate of this order rather than a ruling
authority who imposes it. In 9.1-9 the general character of the
speech and the specific terms 'punishment' and 'recompense'
in v. 7 indicate that the connection between sin and its consequences is seen in the context of a quasi-legal situation in
which the prophet acts as Yahweh's representative in his
dispute with a people who have mistreated his property (the
'land'). This of course fits in well with the use of the term
'indictment' (*rib*) in 4.1 and 12.2.

Fourthly, we need to consider the sociological aspects which
have been detected in the intellectual content of Hosea's message as a challenge to the common political and religious conceptions of his day. Here, as with Utzschneider's work, the
starting-point is not prophecy as an age-old institution of
Israel but the crisis-point in Israelite religion reflected in the
preaching of the eighth-century prophets, including Hosea.
This has been described from many points of view in histories
of Old Testament religion, but it is E.W. Nicholson, building
on the insights of H.H. Schmid on the one hand and Peter
Berger on the other, who has presented a specifically sociological analysis of it. In the background of this study is an
understanding of religion, including early Israelite religion, as
'legitimating the structures and institutions of a society' and
as 'part of a society's endeavour to impose meaning upon its
experience of the world' (Nicholson, *God and his People*, pp.
192-93). In the ancient Near East, and also in Israel before
the rise of classical prophecy, this understanding took the
form of a theology of creation, a 'state-ideology', which is
expressed in myth, in the cult, in wisdom literature and in a
sacral conception of kingship.

Nicholson recognizes that in pre-classical prophecy, and
especially in the case of Elijah, a challenge was mounted to
this way of thinking, but he points out that it was only the
prophets of the eighth century who 'announced Yahweh's
rejection of Israel' and so 'the social order as a whole was

relativized in the face of a radicalized perception of Yahweh's righteousness' (pp. 206-207). What was inaugurated in Israel at this point in Israel was a clash of two opposed 'world-views'; and the Deuteronomists were subsequently to codify and systematize the new insight which they had inherited from the eighth-century prophets. The chief characteristic of this new insight can be described, in terms which largely go back to Weber, as a 'disenchantment *(Entzauberung)* of the world', a 'de-legitimation' of the social order, 'a relativizing of the human world in the face of a transcendent God and his will for righteousness'. Seen in these terms the prophets really did strike at the roots of their contemporaries' existence:

> Therefore I have hewn them by the prophets,
> I have killed them by the words of my mouth (Hos. 6.5).

Nicholson does not elaborate the application of this understanding of prophecy to Hosea, contenting himself with references to Hos. 1.9 and to his criticism of contemporary society in 4.1, 6.6-9, 7.1-7 and 8.3. But it would not be difficult to identify in Hosea's words many expressions of just such a viewpoint. It would also be possible to illustrate from Hosea what Nicholson briefly says about the prophetic understanding of Israel's ultimate destiny:

> Further, because of this 'disenchantment of the world', the world, seen as inimical to God's righteousness, becomes a world not merely to be sustained, as in the cosmogonic religions of antiquity, but a world to be transformed (p. 208).

He several times refers to Jer. 31.31-34 as a classic statement of this idea, but it is of course widely recognized that this passage is but a development of ideas already expressed in other terms in Hos. 2.17-20 and 14.4.

The new insights of eighth-century prophecy have often been presented in a highly individualistic form which finds little basis in the prophetic literature itself. The appreciation of the social dimension of these new ideas which Nicholson has brought to the attention of students of prophecy is a definite step forward, and enables the scale of Hosea's challenge to his contemporaries to be seen more clearly.

Taken alone, however, such an approach is still perhaps

in danger of seeing the prophets too much as isolated individuals, and there is a need for further research to try to explore just how such figures may have been thrown up by the social pressures and tensions of Hosea's time, to which we referred earlier.

Hosea and the Royal Establishment

In conclusion, it is appropriate under the heading of 'Hosea and Society' to consider in more detail than we did in Chapter 2 what was Hosea's attitude to the dominant political institution of his day: the monarchy or royal establishment. This is a subject that is referred to in a number of passages in his book (1.4, 11; 3.4-5; 5.1; 7.3-7; 8.4, 10; 10.3, 7, 15; 13.10-11), but despite this or even because of it scholars have given quite varied accounts of Hosea's teaching. The issue has been clearly put by A. Gelston:

> There can be no doubt that Hosea's attitude to the monarchy of Israel was hostile. But there are at least three ways in which his indictment may be understood. It may refer simply to the actual dissolution of the northern monarchy under a succession of revolutions in Hosea's own time. It may be a far more radical opposition in principle to any form of human kingship over the people of God. Or Hosea's stance may be based on a belief in the 'divine right' of the Davidic dynasty of Judah, coupled with a dismissal of the separate northern monarchy as apostate (p. 71).

In recent years all these views have had their adherents. For example, Gelston himself favours the first view, the second is maintained by Wolff, and the third by Rudolph and G.I. Emmerson. Most of the passages listed above are compatible with any of these views, because they do no more than announce the coming end of kingship in Israel (that is, the northern kingdom) and criticize the people's reliance on their king as a saviour from danger. Hosea does not generally raise deeper questions of political principle, because they were of no concern to him. Two passages, however, do so strongly emphasize the place of human initiative in the appointment of kings as to suggest that Hosea is deliberately challenging a royal ideology which claimed that the monarchy was founded on divine choice and favour.

> They made kings, but not through me;
>   they set up princes, but without my knowledge (8.4).

> Where is now your king, that he may save you?
> Where in all your cities are your rulers, of whom you said,
>   'Give me a king and rulers'?
> I gave you a king in my anger,
>   and I took him away in my wrath (13.10-11).

The first of these passages denies altogether that Yahweh had any part in the appointment of kings and princes. But is this a comprehensive statement that he is opposed to such appointments or, as some would hold, a complaint that he was not consulted about them? In the latter case the implication would be that Yahweh did favour the appointment of those kings and princes whom he indicated as his choice. The second passage speaks of a situation in which the people did apparently appeal to Yahweh to give them a king to 'save' them, and their request was granted, though in an ironic sense: even the provision of the king was an expression of Yahweh's anger and that same anger was to bring about his demise.

In their commentaries Wolff and Mays draw attention to the verbal echo of 1 Sam. 8.6 and suggest that the reference is therefore to the institution of monarchy as such. Wolff finds further support for this view in Hos. 9.15, where the point of the reference to Gilgal may be that it was there that Saul was made king; but the passage is not at all clear. Not all scholars accept that 13.11 is an explicit allusion to 1 Sam. 8.6. Rudolph thinks this is excluded because such a fundamental opposition to monarchic rule on Hosea's part is incompatible with the hope expressed in 1.11. This is a verse to which we shall return below. Gelston and Emmerson point out that the verbs 'gave' and 'took' are Hebrew imperfects and should probably refer to repeated actions of king-making rather than to a single episode in the past, any allusion to 1 Samuel 8 being only implicit. The grammatical argument is, however, not conclusive, as imperfect verbs are sometimes used in poetry to refer to a single past event (e.g. Ps. 81.6-7). Moreover, the difference of the standpoint of 13.10-11 from that of 8.4 is best explained if its reference is to a particular occasion, one different from the contemporary changes of king—an occasion from which the involvement of Yahweh could not be simply excluded. There remains, therefore, good reason to think that in 13.10-11 Hosea grounds his taunt about the weakness of royal rule in the unhappy circumstances of the original introduction of the monarchy. This may not always have been his view, and J. Jeremias has made a good case for seeing a growing severity in Hosea's criticism of the institution of monarchy through chs. 7–13.

If, in his teaching about kingship, Hosea poses a radical challenge to a key aspect of the world-view of his contemporaries, is there any indication of kingship's having a place in his teaching about a future 'transformation', to use Nicholson's term, of the social world? For if there is, then this would be just as decisive a factor for determining Hosea's attitude to kingship as his statements about the past and the present. Two verses seem at first sight to provide evidence of such a view:

> The people of Judah and the people of Israel shall be gathered together and they shall appoint for themselves one head; and they shall take possession of the land, for great shall be the day of Jezreel (1.11).

> Afterward the Israelites shall return and seek the Lord their God, and David their king; they shall come in awe to the Lord and to his goodness in the latter days (3.5).

These two verses have commonly been seen as representing quite different expectations, with 3.5 looking for a straightforward return of the north Israelite tribes to Davidic rule and 1.11 looking for a completely new beginning, in which the term 'head' is deliberately chosen instead of 'king' to show that no mere revival of the discredited monarchy is being envisaged. Wolff, for example, suggests that a return to the charismatic pattern of leadership of the Judges period is in view in 1.11. On the other hand Emmerson has pointed out that, while the term 'head' need not refer to a king, it can do so (1 Sam. 15.17; Ps. 18.43). Probably, therefore, the ideology in the two verses is much the same. The question that remains is whether these statements represent Hosea's own view.

A study of the commentaries shows that most scholars regard the words 'and David their king' (and 'in the latter days') in 3.5 as a later addition made after Hosea's sayings were taken to Judah. Emmerson has contested this common view, suggesting that the phrase is required to complete the picture of restoration implied by the rest of ch. 3, but the central preoccupation of the chapter is in fact with the restored relationship with Yahweh, and the Davidic ideology introduces an alien element into Hosea's message. The recent major commentaries have been more confident about attributing 1.11 to Hosea, but the priority given to Judah together with several features of the context probably indicate a date for this verse too in the sixth century BCE. Clearly one's conclusions about Hosea's ultimate view of kingship are closely bound up with one's judgment about the extent of later redactional activity in the book. Of course if the issue is considered at the level of the prophetic tradition as a whole, it is clear that the book of Hosea has in these verses a contribution to make to a more positive evaluation of political structures, alongside its very negative statements on this subject.

Further Reading

The following general studies of the social character of Israelite prophecy can be consulted for further details and bibliography:

P.L. Berger, 'Charisma and Religious Innovation: The Social Location of Israelite Prophecy', *American Sociological Review* 28 (1963), pp. 940-50.

A.D.H. Mayes, 'Sociology and the Old Testament', in R.E. Clements (ed.), *The World of Ancient Israel* (Cambridge: Cambridge University Press, 1989), pp. 39-63.

A.D.H. Mayes, *The Old Testament in Sociological Perspective* (London: Marshall Pickering, 1989).

R.P. Carroll, 'Prophecy and Society', in Clements, *World*, pp. 203-25.

D.L. Petersen, *The Roles of Israel's Prophets* (JSOTSup, 17; Sheffield: JSOT Press, 1981).

R.R. Wilson, *Prophecy and Society* (Philadelphia: Fortress Press, 1980).

B. Lang, *Monotheism and the Prophetic Minority* (Sheffield: Almond Press, 1983).

E.W. Nicholson, *God and his People* (Oxford: Clarendon Press, 1986), pp. 191-217.

For the theoretical basis of these studies see, e.g.:

P.L. Berger and T. Luckmann, *The Social Construction of Reality* (Harmondsworth: Penguin Books, 1971).

I.M. Lewis, *Ecstatic Religion: An Anthropological Study of Spirit Possession and Shamanism* (Harmondsworth: Penguin Books, 1971).

R. Collins, *Three Sociological Traditions* (Oxford: Oxford University Press, 1985).

An important first attempt to look at Hosea from a sociological point of view influenced by Berger and Luckmann was made in:

H. Utzschneider, *Hosea: Prophet vor dem Ende* (OBO, 31; Freiburg: Universitätsverlag and Göttingen: Vandenhoeck & Ruprecht, 1980).

On the social developments which formed the background to Hosea's activity see:

L. Epzstein, *Social Justice in the Ancient Near East and the People of the Bible* (London: SCM Press, 1986), chs. 3–5.

A. Malamat (ed.), *The Age of the Monarchies: Culture and Society* (The World History of the Jewish People, IV.2; Jerusalem: Massada Press, 1979), pp. 125-46.

On Hosea's view of kingship see especially:

A. Gelston, 'Kingship in the Book of Hosea', *OTS* 19 (1974), pp. 71-85.

G.I. Emmerson, *Hosea. An Israelite Prophet in Judaean Perspective* (JSOTSup, 28; Sheffield: JSOT Press, 1984), pp. 105-13.

5

HOSEA AND HIS RELIGIOUS
BACKGROUND (*GEISTIGE HEIMAT*)

THE PLACE OF THE SO-CALLED INDIVIDUAL or classical prophets within the overall religious life of ancient Israel remains a central topic for discussion in the study of the Old Testament. The poles between which this discussion has moved are well defined in the following question which comes from a recent Cambridge examination paper: 'Did the prophets in Israel develop a distinctive theology of their own, or were they basically exponents of the conventional theological teachings of the great national shrines?' This is a question that will not and should not go away, even though neither of the alternatives which it poses can be said to take account of the issue in its full complexity.

There are different ways of posing the question about the nature of classical prophecy, and they complement one another. Sometimes it has been posed mainly in terms of the attitudes taken up by the prophets towards the religious life of their contemporaries, attitudes that were often very critical; at other times it has been posed rather as a question about their relation to their background and to their predecessors. Here the question will be approached in this second way, though there is of course an originality about the teaching of the classical prophets which distinguishes them from all their contemporaries, even from those with whom they felt some considerable affinity, and some references to this will be made along the way. I have added the German phrase *geistige Heimat* to the title of this chapter deliberately. Hard though it is to translate into English, it defines the subject of the chapter more sharply

than does the English word 'background'. What we are
concerned with is not the religious situation of Hosea's time as
a whole, but rather that part of it which might be said to
constitute his 'spiritual and intellectual home'—a task which
is not only more limited but also more difficult, because it
involves the attempt to be specific about which element or
elements in the wider background were most significant in the
formation of Hosea's message and sayings. The inclusion of
this phrase also serves to stress the importance for any
discussion of this topic of an article entitled 'Hoseas geistige
Heimat' by H.W. Wolff, which was first published in 1956.

Some students of Hosea have seen no need to raise the
question of his religious background, believing that the special
characteristics of his message can be sufficiently explained
from his peculiar psychology, the story of his marriage, or his
own individual insight. But most of those who take this view
are so fascinated by chs. 1–3 that they do not trouble to read
any further, and even in these chapters there are numerous
features which invite comparison with religious movements in
ancient Israel which may have influenced the prophet.

Others have seen the most powerful influence on Hosea to
have been the very tendencies in Israelite religion against
which he protested most strongly: the use of forms of worship
which in his view, whether intentionally or not, amounted to
worship of Baal and other pagan deities. Thus it has been
suggested that the marriage metaphor in ch. 2 is an adaptation, even a caricature, of the mythological idea that Baal was
united in sacral marriage to the earth—an idea, incidentally,
for which there seems to be no evidence in early sources.
Recently a fresh version of this approach has been advocated
by Balz-Cochois (see above, pp. 47-50), who suggests a number
of ways in which Hosea's thinking may have been influenced
by sexual rituals designed to increase fertility, citing especially 2.16-25. She even envisages that Hosea's call to be a
prophet took place while he was witnessing the rituals at a
bamah. She does not, however, regard these as the only
influence on him, but also recognizes the impact of some of
the factors which will be mentioned below.

The majority of the scholars who have considered this question, however, have looked for a more positive dependence of Hosea on some stream of older tradition. Undoubtedly the most popular view has been that he stood in the line of earlier prophets from the northern kingdom, though the idea of a 'prophetic' background was often widened to take in literature and movements that were not 'prophetic' in the strict sense at all, but happened to share some of the viewpoints, mostly critical of the state and its religion, which were also expressed by prophets. The result was that prophecy may have been given more credit than it deserves for initiating correctives to other tendencies in Israelite religion. I believe that the great achievement of Wolff's essay was that almost for the first time, he identified a second group alongside the prophets who, before the rise of classical prophecy, had been the bearers of a conservative tradition which contributed directly to Hosea's message of judgment: the Levites. In fact, somewhat surprisingly, Wolff's view had already been largely anticipated by a scholar who is more usually remembered for his emphasis on the originality and newness of the classical prophets: Bernhard Duhm. In his *Theologie der Propheten*, published in 1875, Duhm wrote, after citing much of the same evidence as is used by Wolff, that Hosea 'could himself have been one of the few Levitical priests who functioned in the northern kingdom and that precisely this experience would provide the most suitable background for Hosea's polemic against the unbridled worship of nature as well as against the increasing proliferation of altars' (pp. 130-31). Wolff himself, incidentally, did not speak of a purely Levite background for Hosea, for he took seriously the indications that Hosea also saw himself as the associate of earlier and contemporary prophets (6.4-6; 9.7-9; 12.8-11). He concluded his essay with these words:

> Through Hosea we begin to comprehend what a powerful movement the Levite-prophetic opposition alliance must have been in the last decades of the northern kingdom, for it to have survived, as a community oriented towards the amphictyony, the storms of the ruin of the state and to have finally led, with the help of Deuteronomy, to quite new developments which continued through the catastrophe that befell Judah and are among the most influential in the history of Israel, not least with respect to Old Testament literature.

The problem with this view, which has no doubt been largely responsible for its failure to be widely accepted, is that it has to envisage a 'very powerful movement' of which no direct trace has remained anywhere in the Old Testament. Particularly in a period when there is now great scepticism about 'communities oriented towards the amphictyony', it is hard to believe that the very prominent elements of tradition in the oracles of Hosea can explained in this way. A similar criticism can be made of the more recent proposal of Morton Smith and B. Lang that Hosea took up the reform programme of a 'Yahweh-alone party' which had its origin in the ninth century. There is therefore good reason to explore a different possibility which was very much in the air in the 1950s when Wolff wrote his essay, but which he seems too quickly to have dismissed. This is that the traditions which Hosea uses and so radically reshapes were already, for the most part, associated together in the cultic traditions of one or more of the major shrines of the northern kingdom.

Hosea and Cultic Tradition

A number of scholars since 1956 have written about Hosea's debt to tradition (see the bibliography), but none of them has given adequate attention to what seems to be direct evidence of some at least of the traditions which were transmitted at the shrines. Before turning to this evidence, however, we should note some general indications in the text of Hosea that he was by no means unaware of the cultic tradition of his people. It has, in the first place, been generally accepted that traditions about the exodus, the wilderness journey and the conquest of the land were transmitted at one or more of the northern shrines, whether in the form of a recital of the stories or in hymns of praise addressed to Yahweh or both. Hosea repeatedly refers to these traditions, and apparently takes it for granted that they are well known to his audience, for example when he speaks of a 'return to Egypt' (8.13; 9.3; 11.5). Then again in 8.2 he indicates his familiarity with the language of public prayer, probably citing phrases from two separate compositions (Wolff):

To me they cry: 'My God', 'we [Israel] know thee'.

The second of these extracts is particularly interesting, because its use of the verb 'know' (*yada‘*) strongly suggests that Hosea's key term 'knowledge of God, knowledge of Yahweh' (2.20; 4.6; 5.4; 6.3, 6 [cf. 11.3, 13.4]) had its origin in the language of the cult. There are several other places where it is probable that Hosea took up the language of public worship in formulating his oracles of judgment (1.6, 9; 2.8-9, 10; 5.14, 15; 6.1; 6.11–7.1; 9.14; 10.15). Even the notion of Yahweh's 'love' (*'ah*^a*bah*) for his people (3.1; 11.1), which many suppose to be an innovation of the prophet himself, can be paralleled in cultic poetry (Ps. 47.5; 78.68; 87.2). Hosea also seems to take for granted the popular view that Yahweh is present in a special sense in the shrines: he uses the expression 'the house of God' without demur (8.1; 9.4, 8, 15; possibly also originally in 6.10), and he regards 'divine absence' as a central aspect of the coming judgment (5.6, 14-15; 9.12). In his prophecies of salvation—if they are his, and some of them probably are—a spoken response to Yahweh by the people is a recurring feature (2.15, 23; 14.2-3), and some details suggest strongly that this was expressed in the form of cultic poetry ('My God' in 2.23; 'words' and 'the fruit of our lips' in 14.2). Another passage, 6.1-3, is probably modelled on a specific form of the priestly summons to worship (cf. Lam. 3.40-42). Although this is often regarded as a citation by Hosea of something of which he does not approve, my own view is that it could well be an authentic part of Hosea's preaching.

We may now look in more detail at one final passage which suggests that Hosea knew and valued traditions transmitted in public worship: 12.2-9. Here Hosea makes specific allusions to features of another major tradition of the northern kingdom, the stories about the patriarch Jacob. This is a difficult passage, which appears to fluctuate between references to the very ambiguous figure of Jacob himself and accusations against the contemporary people of Israel. We may begin our examination with the exhortation in v. 6:

So you, by the help of your God [NRSV has 'to your God', but this is unlikely] return; hold fast to love (*hesed*) and justice (*mišpaṭ*), and wait continually for your God.

Although this looks at first sight like a version of God's
message to the patriarch Jacob in Gen. 28.15, particularly in
view of the reference to 'returning', it is in fact very different
from that passage, above all in its demands for love (*ḥesed*)
and justice (*mišpaṭ*). At the same time it is difficult to regard it
as an original composition of Hosea, as the language is not
(apart from *ḥesed*) really typical of him. The conjunction of
ḥesed and *mišpaṭ* in fact appears in Ps. 101.1, a text which is
normally regarded as a royal, and therefore pre-exilic, psalm.
The words 'wait' and 'continually' are also characteristic of the
devotional language of the Psalms. The possibility therefore
exists that these two lines at least were taken up by Hosea
from some form of cultic instruction. That this is the case
seems to be confirmed if we go back to v. 4, where the
exhortation is located specifically in an encounter with God at
Bethel, which is here for once (contrast 4.15; 10.5) given its
real name by Hosea. The story of Jacob in Genesis 28 seems to
have functioned as the sacred legend (*hieros logos*) of the
Bethel sanctuary, and at the very least Hosea seems here to
be associating the exhortations in v. 6 with this foundation
legend. His argument which follows in vv. 7-9 is then that the
Israel of his day (and indeed for a long time past) has failed to
match the pattern of behaviour that was prescribed in the
traditions of their great national shrine. A small detail adds
some weight to the view that the words of v. 6 formed part of
the contemporary teaching promulgated at the Bethel
sanctuary: in v. 4, the first three lines (stichs) clearly refer to
the patriarch Jacob, but for the fourth the Masoretic text
reads: 'and there he [i.e. God] spoke [or speaks] *with us*'.
Commentators and translators (down to the NRSV) have been
dissatisfied with this, and have found ways, by emendation or
comparative philology, to secure the sense 'with him', a reading already attested in the Septuagint and Peshitta. But may
this not be one of those places where the at first sight less
intelligible reading of the Masoretic text should be retained?
In view of the fluctuation between patriarch and people in this
passage, it is surely entirely natural that, as he approached
the contemporary application of the traditions, Hosea should
have wanted to bring his audience into the picture. If so, then

he is saying that the words which he cites in v. 6 are *still being spoken* by God to his worshippers at Bethel.

A Comparison with Psalms 80 and 81

More direct evidence of the traditions of the northern shrines can, perhaps, be found in certain psalms. It is regrettable that, on the whole, attempts to reconstruct the liturgical form and dominant themes of Israelite worship on the basis of the psalms have tended to pay rather little attention to the date and place at which specific psalms are likely to have been composed and used. This was an understandable reaction against an earlier too historical phase of scholarship, but the result has sometimes been a blurring of distinctions that may need to be made between pre-exilic and postexilic worship and, more relevant here, between the Jerusalem temple and the shrines of the northern kingdom. Although by far the greater part of the Psalter is no doubt Judaean in origin, and all of it presumably owes its preservation to the Jewish communities of postexilic times, there seem to be some psalms whose composition should be placed in the northern kingdom, prior to its fall in 722 BCE. Such psalms may be able to shed valuable light on the form and content of worship at shrines such as Bethel, Gilgal and Dan, and so provide a basis for determining the extent to which Hosea's preaching was indebted to liturgical traditions.

Two useful pointers to the identification of such northern psalms would seem to be the following:

a. negatively, the absence of two themes which we know to have been distinctively characteristic of Judaean worship—the election of the Davidic dynasty and the special place of Jerusalem and its temple;
b. positively, reference to the nation by the name 'Joseph', since it is clear from a number of passages that this was, like Hosea's preferred term 'Ephraim', a name applied specifically to the northern kingdom (cf. Ps. 78.67; Ezek. 37.19; Amos 5.15).

On this basis three psalms, interestingly placed close together in the Psalter, emerge as likely candidates for a north Israelite origin: 77, 80 and 81. For the sake of brevity, only Psalms 80 and 81 will be considered here. The name 'Joseph' occurs in 80.1 and 81.5. In 80.2 there is additional evidence of a northern origin in the naming of three northern tribes— Ephraim, Benjamin and Manasseh—as those for whom Yahweh's aid is sought. In fact, it may be legitimate to use these names as a chronological indicator as well, since it was the territories of these three tribes which remained under nominally independent Israelite rule after 733 or 732, when the territories of the Galilean and Transjordanian tribes were incorporated into the Assyrian empire. This would place the composition of Psalm 80 within what are likely to have been the later years of Hosea's prophetic activity.

In these Psalms there are a number of themes which correspond closely to central features of Hosea's own teaching:

(a) Both psalms affirm that Israel is Yahweh's own 'people' (80.4; 81.8, 11, 13): cf. Hos. 6.11, 11.7 and, negated, 1.9 etc.

(b) Both, equally, trace this relationship back to the exodus from Egypt (80.8; 81.5-7, 10), and refer to Yahweh's care for Israel in other events of her early history: the wilderness journey (80.1; 81.7) and the settlement in Canaan (80.9-11, 15). Compare e.g. Hos. 13.4-6, where the divine self-introduction in 13.4 is verbally very close to that in Ps. 81.10.

(c) Ps. 80 is dominated by the imagery of Israel as a flock of sheep and a vine, which Hosea also uses (4.16; 10.1; 14.7 [cf. 9.10]).

(d) Both psalms imply that it is Yahweh who is the giver of physical nourishment to Israel (80.1; 81.10, 16) and their protector against their enemies (80.3-7, 12; 81.14-15). Hosea takes up the first of these themes in ch. 2, while the second seems to lie behind his criticism of reliance on military might (8.14; 10.13).

(e) Psalm 80 includes a prayer for the reigning king, although the allusive language used has often obscured this. But in v. 17 'the man at your right hand' and 'the son of man whom you have made strong for yourself' can scarcely be anyone else in view of the similar Judaean court language in Ps. 110.1 and 89.21. Kingship is also of course a preoccupation of Hosea, and some of his remarks indicate the high regard in which the king was held (13.10).

(f) Finally, in this review of details, there is the demand in Ps. 81.9 that Israel should worship no God but Yahweh. This corresponds to what might be called the dominant theme of Hosea, that Israel has turned away from Yahweh to worship Baal and other deities and so merits divine punishment (see especially ch. 2, but also e.g. 13.4-6, where as in the psalm it is apostasy from the God of the exodus that is specifically mentioned).

Having established that the contents of these two psalms show much resemblance to Hosea, I should like to take the comparison a little further by considering them as whole compositions, each with its distinct religious character. Both of them, we may first note, are likely to have been used in public worship: Psalm 80 is a community lament, with a refrain in vv. 3, 7 and 19, while the hymnic introduction to Psalm 81, with its typical plural imperatives, again presupposes the presence of a congregation. But in their theological outlook they are actually rather different, and sufficiently so for us to reckon with a different relationship between each of them and Hosea. Psalm 80 makes its plea to Yahweh in a time of trouble, perhaps the Assyrian invasions, on the basis of the election traditions, past history and the divine choice of the king: this is precisely the basis for security which Hosea repeatedly challenges. In other words, although Hosea takes up some of his themes from this kind of tradition, he is not at all close to its underlying spirit and he is free to reshape it into something quite new. A further example of this can perhaps be seen on the level of imagery. In Ps. 80 Israel's enemies, from whom Yahweh is expected to save them, are portrayed as wild animals (v. 13): is it this, turned around, which lies behind Hosea's bold portrayal of Yahweh himself as a wild animal (5.14; 6.1; 13.7-8)?

Psalm 81 begins in an even more confident way, calling for celebration at the regular festivals and praise of God, who is 'our strength' or possibly 'our defence' (v. 1) and 'the God of Jacob' (vv. 1 and 4). But the prophetic oracle in v. 6-16 is much more critical of the people. After citing in an allusive, poetic way some elements of the *Heilsgeschichte*, it turns to rebuke, based on the demand for exclusive worship of Yahweh mentioned above. It concludes with a call to repentance, promising that *if* this is forthcoming, *then* Yahweh will subdue Israel's enemies and provide them with abundant crops (vv. 13-16). This is not identical with the characteristic preaching of Hosea, which states that Israel has refused and is in fact unable to repent (5.4), that cultic worship is to be brought to an end (2.11; 9.1-6); and that defeat and devastation are unavoidable. Nevertheless, it is close to Hosea's teaching, and it is plausible to suggest that it is out of such cultic prophecy that Hosea's much more radical message developed. His very complaint that the people will not repent presupposes some such preaching, and his references to earlier prophets very likely include it within their scope (cf. 6.5; 9.8 [cf. 'in the house of his God'!]; 12.10, 13). In fact there is a little evidence that Hosea's own preaching began with such an eleventh-hour message (2.2-3), before he began to proclaim unconditional doom (see Chapter 2 above).

Hosea did not remain tied to this message of unconditional doom to the very end of his prophetic activity. As doom steadily overtook Israel, the very personal way in which he had come to understand Israel's relationship to Yahweh and her offence against him made it impossible for him to believe that this was really the end. What is interesting is that in this situation he went back to the old cultic traditions, and spoke, on the basis of his confidence in Yahweh's freedom and love as expressed in them, of a new and better beginning. The exodus and associated traditions played an important part here, and we can see this in 11.1-11 and in 2.14-15. But so, it seems, did the perception of Yahweh as the true giver of the fertility of the land, of which we see only traces in Psalms 80 and 81. Passages like 2.21-23, 6.1-3 and 14.5-8, may also, if our argument about Hosea's debt to cultic tradition is accepted, have been based on texts from this source which are now lost. To this extent we may agree with Robert Murray's contention (see bibliography) that Hosea knew and used a 'creation-based' tradition from the cult as well as the historical tradition of the exodus. The 'cosmic covenant' passage in ch. 2, however, is a less secure basis from which to argue such a case, as it seems to be, like some other verses in Hos. 1–2, more closely related to sixth-century developments in prophecy, and is probably not by Hosea.

The scholars who have come closest to the view put forward here are M.J. Buss and H.P. Nasuti. Buss's article on the Psalms of Asaph and Korah indicates his support for the view that Psalms 77, 80 and 81 were north Israelite in origin; and in his book on Hosea he favoured a cultic background for some features of Hosea's oracles. But he seems not to have thought of exploring the connections between the specific north Israelite texts and Hosea's words. In effect he claims both more and less than I should wish to do. Nasuti's recent book is on tradition-history and the psalms of Asaph. As a pupil of R.R. Wilson he has a lot to say about the 'Ephraimite' tradition-stream which includes, in his opinion, both Hosea and the Asaph psalms as a whole, and he notes a few specific connections between Hosea and Psalms 80 and 81. But he is reluctant to distinguish as I would wish to do between northern and Judaean compositions within this group of psalms, and as a result he does not make any claims about the dependence of Hosea upon cultic traditions.

The argument of this chapter is not intended to contradict scholars such as Wolff and Brueggemann who have argued for the dependence of Hosea on legal tradition or priestly tradition. It has been rather to suggest that in Psalms 80 and 81 we have evidence of the confluence of these traditions at one or more north Israelite shrines, and that various characteristics of Hosea's language and message make it likely that it was from such a cultic source that he derived his knowledge of tradition.

Further Reading

The general thesis that the classical prophets were developing the traditions which were at the centre of pre-exilic Israelite worship is maintained, for example, in:

G. von Rad, *Old Testament Theology*, II (Edinburgh: Oliver & Boyd, 1965) (= *The Message of the Prophets* [London: SCM Press, 1968]).

R.E. Clements, *Prophecy and Covenant* (London: SCM Press, 1965).

R. Murray, *The Cosmic Covenant: Biblical Themes of Justice, Peace and the Integrity of Creation* (London: Sheed & Ward, 1992).

Wolff's essay, 'Hoseas geistige Heimat' (which has not been translated into English) was published in *TLZ* 81 (1956), pp. 83-94 and is reprinted in his *Gesammelte Schriften I* (Munich: Chr. Kaiser, 1964, 2nd edn 1973), pp. 232-50. For a summary see the English translation of his commentary on Hosea, pp. xxii-xxiii, 79-81, 121, 144-146. Wolff's view was partly anticipated by B. Duhm, *Die Theologie der Propheten als Grundlage für die innere Entwicklungsgeschichte der israelitischen Religion* (Bonn: A. Marcus, 1875).

For the idea of a 'Yahweh-alone party' to which Hosea attached himself see:
Morton Smith, *Palestinian Parties that Shaped the Old Testament* (London: SCM Press, 2nd edn, 1987), ch. 2.
B. Lang, *Monotheism and the Prophetic Minority* (Sheffield: Almond Press, 1983), ch. 1 (pp. 30-36 deal with Hosea).

Among other studies devoted to Hosea in particular the following are especially relevant to this chapter:
W. Brueggemann, *Tradition for Crisis* (Atlanta: John Knox Press, 1968).
M.J. Buss, *The Prophetic Word of Hosea* (BZAW, 111; Berlin: de Gruyter, 1969).
G.I. Emmerson, *Hosea. An Israelite Prophet in Judaean Perspective* (JSOTSup, 28; Sheffield: JSOT Press, 1984), pp. 124-38.
D.R. Daniels, *Hosea and Salvation History* (BZAW, 191; Berlin: de Gruyter, 1990).

On the Asaphite psalms, which include those discussed here, see:
M.J. Buss, 'The Psalms of Asaph and Korah', *JBL* 82 (1963), pp. 382-92.
H.P. Nasuti, *Tradition-History and the Psalms of Asaph* (SBLDS, 88; Atlanta: Scholars Press, 1988).

6

HOSEA'S MARRIAGE

UNTIL COMPARATIVELY MODERN TIMES the dominant view was that chs. 1–3 of Hosea are not accounts of Hosea's real dealings with one or more women, but rather that they are accounts of visionary experiences or parables serving only to convey a message about the spiritual relationship between God and Israel (or in Christian circles between God and the Christian church). There were occasional instances of a literal interpretation—for example in a Talmudic passage (*B. Pes.* 87a-b) the command to marry a prostitute in 1.2 is understood as a divine ploy to soften Hosea's harsh message of judgment, since after the birth of his three children God commands him to divorce his wife, and his reluctance teaches him that God too has no intention of abandoning his people. But a symbolic reading is more typical, as in the Targum, where the taking of Gomer and the birth of the children are no more than a symbol standing for preaching against sinful Israel, and ch. 3 is represented as entirely a speech of God to Hosea about his love for his wayward people. Such views have survived into modern times, but they have been held by only a minority of modern scholars.

Until about 1960 the modern discussion centred on the questions of whether the woman in ch. 3 is Gomer or not and, if she is, whether ch. 1 (in particular vv. 2-3) and ch. 3 are different accounts of the same event or, as has been more commonly held, accounts of two different events in Hosea's relationship with his wife (on this debate see the article by H.H. Rowley). No final resolution of this problem has been achieved, although the view that Gomer is the woman

referred to in ch. 3 and that ch. 1 and ch. 3 relate to different
episodes appears to have predominated (so Rowley and, in
addition to those mentioned in his survey, Weiser, Wolff, von
Rad and Mays). But the view that ch. 3 is not about Gomer
has been maintained recently by G. Fohrer and by Rudolph,
to whom we shall return, and the view that ch. 1 and ch. 3
are, at least in part, parallel accounts of the same events has
been taken by scholars such as O. Eissfeldt, J. Lindblom,
P.R. Ackroyd and H. McKeating.

Rudolph's Redaction-Critical Approach

In the past twenty-five years the discussion of this problem,
like that of many others in Old Testament study, has been
marked by much greater attention to the possibility that later
redactors have played a major part in fashioning the canon-
ical form of the narratives. Earlier scholars had identified
several verses or parts of verses in chs. 1–3 which they
thought unlikely to be from Hosea himself (1.1, 7; 1.10–2.1;
and some phrases in 3.5; see further Chapter 7), but this
made little or no difference to the main outline of the narratives. Only occasionally was it suggested that, for example,
the occurrences of $z^e nunim$ ('whoredom') in 1.2b were unoriginal, and Rowley's jibe that this involved 'the familiar expedi-
ent of surgery' to dispose of 'inconvenient words' probably
reflected a widespread suspicion of such an approach.

But the publication of Rudolph's German commentary on
Hosea in 1966 seems to have been responsible for a noticeable
shift in scholarly evaluation of these chapters. His views
therefore deserve careful attention. They are set out in two
sections of his commentary in which he vigorously and
sometimes quite playfully debates with many previous
scholars who have written on the problem. He first outlines,
and refutes, the various older views which were referred to in
the opening paragraph of this chapter, characterizing them as
above all attempts to clear Yahweh of the charge that he
demanded something immoral of Hosea in commanding him
to marry an *'ešet $z^e nunim$* ('a woman of whoredom'—1.2). He
then considers and rejects the view that $z^e nunim$ here means

not literal prostitution but, symbolically, the religious apostasy that was rife in the northern kingdom at the time, so that Gomer was a perfectly respectable woman who, like most of her contemporaries, followed the wrong religion. Rudolph's main objection to this is that it substitutes an actual demonstration of contemporary apostasy (it is assumed that Hosea could not find a devout worshipper of Yahweh) for a symbolic action, and this is out of keeping with the rest of the chapter. This view is somewhat similar to that of Wolff, with which Rudolph deals at greater length. Wolff believes, as we have already seen in Chapter 3, that in Hosea's time Israelite brides were forced to serve as cultic prostitutes, and that *'ešet z^{e}nunim* was an appropriate term to use for a woman who had been or would be subjected to such rituals. Rudolph is able to show that none of the evidence to which Wolff appeals, either biblical or extrabiblical, is adequate to prove the existence of such a custom in Israel and that two passages in Deuteronomy (22.13-21, 23-29) are evidence against it, or at least against its being prevalent in Hosea's time.

A more widespread view is that the term *'ešet z^{e}nunim* was applied to Gomer with hindsight: that is, that in retelling the story of Hosea's family life the prophet or his disciples (the narrative is composed in the third person) inserted it because it reflected the way that Gomer eventually turned out, so that her story could readily serve as an illustration of Hosea's message about Israel's 'whoredom'. The same interpretation of the story, in essence, is adopted by those who make the designation of Gomer as a prostitute 'proleptic' (so J. Wellhausen, W.R. Harper and others). To this Rudolph objects, very forcefully, that if Gomer did desert Hosea for another man it is most remarkable that the narrator did not say so, in view of the potential of such behaviour for strengthening the parallel between Hosea's marriage and Israel's relationship with Yahweh. It is also very difficult to give *'ešet z^{e}nunim* the sense required by this interpretation.

Rudolph then considers two views which take the narrative of ch. 1 at face value and accept that Hosea knowingly married a woman who was already a prostitute. Some have sought to explain this remarkable behaviour (and its sequel) psychoanalytically, but as Rudolph points out, such efforts are far too speculative to carry conviction, and some of the details of the theory are also implausible. More probable than this is the view, represented for example by Rowley, that Hosea felt constrained by a power outside himself, which he recognized as Yahweh, to act in this way, just as other prophets felt constrained to act in ways scarcely less scandalous, in order to portray contemporary situations that were no less shocking to them. But Rudolph rejects this view too, not so much because he thinks that it would have been immoral of Yahweh to have commanded it as because it would have been self-defeating. He pictures Hosea's contemporaries, on being offered the prophetic explanation of this remarkable lapse from decency, responding with a taunt: 'So, the fact that you share your bed with a slut is all for the sake of our religious education! Dear Hosea, save your speeches and don't take us for fools! *We* know the real truth: it just suited you to do it, and now you are covering up your pleasure in sex by quoting a divine command.' (p. 46). Not the best way to establish a prophet's authority, he suggests!

A further difficulty for this view, he says, is that it creates an inconsistency between the symbol and what it stands for, since when Yahweh 'married' Israel she was still pure and faithful (cf. 9.10; 11.1), unlike Gomer. Moreover, the symbolic marriage is the only instance in the Old Testament of a prophetic symbolic action representing an existing state of affairs rather than a future event. This latter point leads Rudolph to suggest that the symbolic interpretation of Hosea's marriage is not an original feature of the account but was imposed on it later. He thinks that this is confirmed by two further observations:

1. The wording of the divine command as it stands is problematic. The use of *qah* ('take') with two coordinated objects ('a wife' and 'children') either implies that the prostitute was to bring some children already born with her (which is contrary to the narrative which follows) or that the reader is supposed to supply a verb like 'beget' with the second object (which is bad Hebrew). In any case, he says, *yalde z*^{e}*nunim* does not mean 'children born of a prostitute' but 'children with an

inclination to immorality', and it was not a foregone conclusion that the children to be born would follow the morals of their mother rather than those of their father.

2. The character of the children plays no part in what follows, and neither does that of their mother. All the emphasis falls on the children's names.

Consequently, Rudolph concludes, the text of v. 2b cannot now be in its original form. It must originally have read something like the following: 'The Lord said to Hosea, Take for yourself a wife, so that she may bear you children.' The present form of the text must be due to the compiler of chs. 1–3, who according to Rudolph deduced from 2.2ff. that Hosea's marital life and Yahweh's relationship with Israel ran parallel and so inserted the references to whoredom into 1.2 to make this clear. But the compiler was mistaken, and in reality Gomer was blameless.

Rudolph returns to the debate in his introduction to ch. 3, where he deals both with the interpretation (and redactional history) of that chapter and with its relationship to ch. 1. Unfortunately these two aspects of his argument are somewhat intertwined, and it will be easier to follow it if we attempt to disentangle them. First his interpretation and analysis of ch. 3. The main distinctive features are the following:

a) Rudolph takes 'again' (*'od*) in v. 1 with 'said' rather than with 'go', claiming that the Masoretic punctuation leaves both possibilities open. This then looks back to the previous occurrence of 'the Lord said' in 1.2.

b) He argues that 'her' in v. 2 need not imply that some specific person previously mentioned is meant, since there are cases in biblical Hebrew where an object suffix refers back to an indefinite noun: he cites Isa. 46.7b and Lam. 3.34, to which Lam. 3.36 might be added. His translation is: 'So I bought *one* for myself...', i.e. a woman of the kind described above.

c) Why did Hosea have to pay? Rudolph rejects the view of many commentators that the mixed payment in cash and kind adds up to the equivalent of thirty shekels of silver, the price of a slave according to Exod. 21.32 (compare also Lev. 27.4). He argues, with some justice, that the basis for the calculation is dubious in several respects. Since the chapter gives (according to him) no encouragement to the idea that a marriage was being undertaken—it says 'love', not 'take as wife', in v. 1—he also rejects the view that a bride-price is involved. What then? 'What Hosea in fact does here, or purports to do [see below], is something which has constantly recurred in the history of human relations in all times and peoples, namely that a man keeps a girl and pays her, so as to have her entirely at his disposal for a definite time' (p. 92).

d) But what can have been in Hosea's mind as he did this? Here Rudolph takes an unusual view. Most commentators, whoever they think the woman was, take the references to 'love' in v. 1 at their face value, or at least assign them to a redactor if they find this impossible. But Rudolph asks what kind of love is represented by the treatment of the woman in v. 3 and of Israel in v. 4? The usual answer has been that these deprivations are only temporary, designed to prepare for a full relationship of intimacy later, as v. 5 indicates. But Rudolph regards the whole of v. 5 as secondary, so for him, or rather for Hosea, there is no light at the end of the tunnel. Consequently he feels driven to understand 'love' in an ironic sense: (Yahweh's 'love') 'consists in the fact that he deprives Israel of all that was previously of value to her, in other words, *'aheb* [the Hebrew word for 'love'] is here used ironically and v. 1b does not mean the indestructible love of Yahweh, but has a threatening sense. Only so do we arrive at a consistent interpretation of vv. 1-4.' Hosea's love for the woman is to be of the same kind. The chapter in its original form was all about punishment.

Now we may look, much more briefly, at Rudolph's view of the relationship of this chapter to ch. 1. On the theological level he sees it as very close, since on his understanding both chapters originally spoke of unqualified judgment. But on the biographical level, he holds, there is no connection: the woman in ch. 3 is not Gomer, but a prostitute whose name is not given. His main arguments for this are as follows:

a) On Rudolph's understanding of ch. 1, Gomer was not a prostitute, as was the woman of ch. 3—she was of exemplary character.

b) The common view that in the course of the events described in ch. 1, or after them, Gomer was unfaithful to Hosea is pure speculation. Surely such a lapse would have been mentioned in the narrative, since it would be highly relevant to the symbolism of the events as they are usually reconstructed.

c) If Gomer is meant, why does the Hebrew of 3.1 not speak (as the NIV has boldly but inaccurately done) of 'your wife' instead of the indefinite 'a woman'?

d) The threatening character of ch. 3 does not allow it to function, as it usually does on the common view, as the vehicle of a message which superseded the message of doom in ch. 1.

To summarize: on the biographical level Rudolph holds that Hosea married Gomer, a woman of respectable character, and had by her three children, to whom he gave symbolic names to convey his message of judgment against Israel. He also (as far as I can see Rudolph never commits himself as to whether this took place before or after the marriage to Gomer) bought a prostitute and locked her up in his house, to symbolize the same message of judgment. Rudolph does not deny Hosea a message of salvation elsewhere, but he holds that it was in no way intentionally represented in Hosea's relations with these women.

Some commentators who have written since Rudolph's commentary was published in 1966 have paid little attention to this aspect of it. Of those who have interacted at length with Rudolph, one (A. Deissler) has rejected his interpretation of ch. 1 in favour of the more traditional approach of Wolff, two (R.E. Clements and J. Schreiner) follow him quite closely on both chapters, and a third (J. Jeremias) agrees with him on ch. 1 and on the secondary character of 3.5, but takes an entirely different and much more traditional view of the rest of ch. 3, which has, like the common view, to assume that Gomer was at some stage unfaithful to Hosea but was taken back by him as a symbol of Yahweh's unquenchable love for Israel.

Critique of Rudolph's Theory

There are, in my opinion, serious weaknesses in some of
Rudolph's arguments. To begin with ch. 3, where he has found
least support, the idea that Hosea's purchase of a woman
refers to the hiring of a mistress is most unlikely. Hosea knew
very well what the word for that was (cf. 2.12; 8.9-10; 9.1).
'Bought' implies a once-and-for-all payment. Its significance
here remains somewhat uncertain, but M.J. Geller's
observation that ch. 3 contains several features which suggest
a marriage contract may well be on the right lines. Again,
Rudolph's 'ironic' interpretation of 'love' is very hard to
accept. Elsewhere Hosea does not employ this kind of irony,
which is more typical of Amos; rather he states plainly that
Yahweh has ceased to love Israel (1.6, 9.15). And what of the
other occurrences of *'aheb* in 3.1? Are they ironical? Surely
not. Hosea would have had a hard time trying to understand
Yahweh's command if it were intended in the sense Rudolph
suggests. Even if v. 5 is to be regarded as secondary, there is
nothing in vv. 3-4 which is incompatible with an ultimately
loving intention. It is best to take *'aheb* in its straightforward
sense, and see the measures in vv. 3-4 as designed for
punishment and correction, but not repudiation.

Rudolph's view of 1.2b is based largely on alleged difficulties
in having Hosea's marriage to a prostitute symbolize Israel's
unfaithfulness to Yahweh. But are the difficulties really so
great? It is possible that Rudolph makes the same mistake as
that which he criticizes in others, by trying to look too closely
into what was psychologically possible in a prophet's con-
sciousness. Perhaps marrying a prostitute was, from a
communicative point of view, not a very successful piece of
prophetic symbolism, and brought the prophet mockery
rather than a patient hearing, but the same seems to be true of
other examples of prophetic symbolism, and it does not mean
that Hosea could not have thought that it was the right thing
for him to do. The fact that this seems to be the only instance
of a prophetic symbolic action representing a state rather than
a future event is worth noting, but can we be so sure that
Hosea would not have turned this traditional prophetic

practice to his own purpose? The so-called inconsistency between sign and thing signified only applies if one demands that the two correspond at all points, and that is by no means typical of prophetic symbolism in general. There is perhaps more force in Rudolph's two supporting observations, but it is not clear that they require that 1.2b has been worked over by a redactor. In one respect they seem to proceed from a mistaken premiss, for Rudolph states that 'children of har-lotry' (*yalde z^{e}nunim*) does not mean 'children born of a harlot' but 'children who themselves get a tendency to immorality'. On the contrary it is perfectly possible that it means 'children born of a union with a prostitute'.

There is one argument that has been used to support editorial intervention in 1.2b; it is, however, used not by Rudolph himself but by Schreiner and Jeremias. This is that the language of the final clause of the verse is Deuteronomistic. The key phrase for this argument is *me'ah^{a}re yhwh*, 'by forsaking the Lord', which immediately follows the verb *zanah*, 'commits...whoredom'. However, this precise form of words is in fact never found in Deuteronomistic literature, nor anywhere else in the Old Testament. There are examples of other verbs being followed by *me'ah^{a}re* and of *zanah* followed by *'ah^{a}re* and an expression like 'other gods', but this particular phrase is unique. Moreover, since *me'ah^{a}re* itself occurs regularly in, for example, the old narratives of 1 and 2 Samuel, there is no particular reason to ascribe the composite expression here specifically to the Deuteronomists. The metaphorical use of *zanah* in other combinations is of course well-attested in Hosea (cf. 4.12 [*mittah̠at* ^{e}*lohehem*] and 9.1 [*me'al* ^{e}*loheyka*]).

A New Possibility?

Can we then go back to the 'traditional' view which basically holds that Gomer was or became a bad lot but that Hosea took her back as a symbol of Yahweh's enduring love for Israel? I do not believe that we can. To begin with, although chs. 1–3 as they stand may give the impression of being a single, unified story, this impression is not confirmed by a careful study of the book of Hosea as a whole. In the light of the overall development of Hosea's message (see Chapter 2 above) I have already argued that, while ch. 1 reflects a very early stage in Hosea's ministry c.750 BCE, the events of ch. 3 cannot be much earlier than 730, and may be as late as 720. Now it is still possible on this view that the same woman is meant in ch. 3 as in ch. 1, but this identification is by no means as compelling as if we assume, as I suspect most people do, that the events of ch. 3 followed fairly closely on those of ch. 1.

Further, some of Rudolph's criticisms of the usual view hold good. In particular it is difficult to understand why no explicit reference is made to Gomer's supposed desertion of Hosea, and it is difficult to explain the indefinite 'a woman' in 3.1 if Hosea's own unfaithful wife is meant—after all, given those instructions, Hosea might have gone after the wrong one! Rudolph has also exposed the weakness of many previous treatments of the phrases 'a wife of harlotry' and, more especially, 'children of harlotry' in 1.2, although his own explanation of them is no more satisfactory. On the other hand, I do not think that the argument over the syntactical connection of 'again' in 3.1 adds anything to the argument between Rudolph and the more traditional view, as both interpretations remain equally possible whichever verb it modifies. All that the 'again' excludes is the third main alternative, that ch. 1 and ch. 3 are different accounts of the same event.

I did not expect, when I began work on a commentary on Hosea some years ago, to find anything new to say about Hosea's marriage—the ground has been well trodden, and I was convinced that it is more important to grasp the prophetic teaching of chs. 1–3 than to attempt to unscramble Hosea's private life. But to my surprise a possibility emerged which, it seems to me, can deal with the difficulties raised by Rudolph without the need for the far-reaching and unconvincing theories about redactional activity which he and his followers have adopted. Let us look again, then, at 1.2-3. What, first of all, do the phrases a 'wife of harlotry' and 'children of harlotry' mean? Rudolph has reviewed a number of suggestions about the meaning of the first and shown their weaknesses, but at the end he leaves it unresolved whether the reference is to a

prostitute (of whatever kind) or to a woman with an inclination to immorality (p. 49). It seems to me that the idea of an
inclination has to be artificially imported into the text. The
unique phrase may well be a simple equivalent to 'whore'
(*zonah*, which is sometimes preceded by *'iššah*). One could
compare the numerous phrases where 'a man of' (Heb. *'iš*)
and similar expressions are combined with an abstract to
describe a settled attribute. 'Whoredom' is a favourite word of
Hosea's: he uses it more than it is used in any other Old
Testament book (cf. 2.2, 4; 4.12; 5.4), and he may have deliberately avoided the normal word for prostitute here to secure
the parallel with 'children of whoredom'. If a distinction is to
be drawn between a 'whore' and a 'wife/woman of whoredom',
the latter would have to apply to a woman who actually
engaged in immoral practices, i.e. took money for sex,
although she was not 'professionally' a prostitute. There is no
reason to think that it could be used of a woman who merely
had a so far latent tendency in that direction. When it comes
to 'children of whoredom' Rudolph opts firmly for the render-
ing 'children with an inclination towards immorality' (p. 47).
But the expression must again indicate a real and not just a
potential connection with 'whoredom'. Since the meaning
'child prostitute' is not very likely, it probably refers to the
occasion of their birth (cf. 'the son of his old age' in Gen. 37.3,
and 'the wife of your youth' in Mal. 2.14) and indicates that
they were to be born of the sexual union of a man with a
prostitute. Others who take this view suppose that the man in
question was not Hosea but someone else, who was the father
of Gomer's second and third children (the first is said to have
been Hosea's own—cf. 'him' in 1.3). But against this is the
fact, to which Rudolph has drawn attention, that the narrative nowhere says that Gomer was unfaithful to Hosea.

There is in fact an alternative possibility, which requires no
invention of extra details in the story. This is that the man in
question was Hosea himself: but if Gomer was his wife, their
children would surely not merit such a disparaging designation. But *was* Gomer his wife? Commentators have usually
assumed that the use of 'take' (Heb. *laqah*) in vv. 2-3 reflects
the common idiom for taking a wife. But, as noted above, the

most likely interpretation of 'children of whoredom' does not
fit in with this very well. It may also be pointed out that the
full expression for a marriage is '(He) took (her) to be his
wife', which does not occur here, and so the meaning 'married'
is not obligatory. One possible alternative is 'get', for which
laqaḥ is quite often used, but a specifically sexual alternative
also exists. In Leviticus 20 (see vv. 14, 17 and 21) *laqaḥ* seems
to be used interchangeably with 'lie with' (Heb. *šakab 'im*) as
an expression for sexual intercourse, irrespective of whether
there is a legal marriage. So the meaning of Hos. 1.2 may be:
'Take (in a sexual sense) a prostitute and get children born of
whoredom'. This makes very good sense of the passage as a
whole. The symbolism is very plausible, though it is not that
with which we are familiar. Gomer still stands for Israel; but
Hosea, as one of her clients, now stands not for Yahweh, but
for Baal, one of Israel's clients, or 'lovers', as Hosea calls them.
An act of straightforward prostitution was in fact the best
symbol for what is described in the last line of Hos. 1.2, since
on the normal view, as Rudolph pointed out, marriage would
symbolize only the beginning of Yahweh's relationship, not
the corruption of it which is actually mentioned.

What of ch. 3? The first point is that we are not bound to see
the woman as being Gomer. If, as suggested above, Hosea
and Gomer were not married, the usual story-line with its
neat parallel between Yahweh–Israel and Hosea–Gomer has
already been broken down. The time-lapse between ch. 1 and
ch. 3 is also against the identification, and the indefinite 'a
woman' in 3.1 favours the view that Hosea is to set out and
find another corrupt woman. The fact that she is married (she
has committed adultery) rules out Gomer, unless we suppose
that she married someone else and then was unfaithful to
him, after the events of ch. 1; but there is no evidence of this.

There are therefore two separate symbolic actions, involving
different promiscuous women. They represent two entirely
different situations: the first, introduced by 'take' (1.2) stands
for the improper association of Israel with Baal, while the
second, introduced by 'love', stands for Yahweh's seeking out
of faithless Israel. On the level of what is symbolized there is
continuity, on the biographical level there is not. The exact

circumstances in which Hosea 'bought' the unnamed woman of ch. 3 are elusive, and no great confidence can be placed in any of the theories. Geller's view that the payment was a *mohar* or bride-price is attractive, partly because it provides an apt parallel to the passage about betrothal in 2.19-20.

It is largely ch. 2 which is responsible for what I take to be a widespread misreading of ch. 1 and ch. 3. Chapter 2 portrays the whole relationship between Yahweh and Israel as a marriage broken and restored, and the narratives which flank it have been assumed to combine to make a similar story. It may seem that ch. 2 only makes sense if Hosea's marriage, separation and reconciliation were there in the background to suggest the pattern. But this is not so. It is important to remember that, for all its continuity of imagery, ch. 2 includes several sharp transitions and even an outright contradiction, and the different stages of its composition can be plausibly related to Hosea's developing message as it can be reconstructed and related to historical events on the basis of chs. 4–14. The earliest section is probably 2.2-3, in which the prophet is still pleading with the people to abandon their apostasy and so escape Yahweh's vengeance. In the following section, 2.4-5, 8-13, certain judgment is decreed against the wayward people. This corresponds to the message conveyed in ch. 1. Hos. 2.2-3 are therefore earlier than ch. 1. But these verses already employ the image of the unfaithful wife who has turned to prostitution: in other words, this image was devised prior to the events described in ch. 1 and is not dependent upon them. When ch. 2 was gradually enlarged, so that it extended beyond the situation symbolized in 1.2-9, it was natural that it should have been put in second place, and so ch. 1 became what 1.2, translated literally, calls 'the beginning of Yahweh's speaking through Hosea' (compare p. 107 below). But it was not really so. In fact, so far as we can understand such things, the symbolic action was probably suggested to the prophet by the image which he had already used in his summons to repentance. Where then did he get the image from? Was it from tradition, or by a parody of the myth of the sacred marriage? These are possibilities. But it may have come from his own fertile imagination, which has given us so many other memorable images.

Further Reading

The classic account of the problems surrounding Hosea's marriage is:

H.H. Rowley, 'The Marriage of Hosea', *BJRL* 39 (1956–57), pp. 200-23 (reprinted in his *Men of God* [Edinburgh and London: Nelson, 1963], pp. 66-97).

For more recent adherents of the views discussed by Rowley see the commentaries of Weiser, Wolff, Mays and McKeating and:

P.R. Ackroyd, in *Peake's Commentary on the Bible* (ed. M. Black and H.H. Rowley; London: Nelson, rev. edn, 1962), p. 603.

J. Lindblom, *Prophecy in Ancient Israel* (Oxford: Basil Blackwell, 1962), pp. 165-69.

O. Eissfeldt, *The Old Testament: An Introduction* (Oxford: Basil Blackwell, 1965) (ET of *Das Alte Testament: Eine Einleitung* [Tübingen: Mohr, 3rd edn, 1964]), pp. 387-90.

G. von Rad, *Old Testament Theology*, II, pp. 140-41 (*The Message of the Prophets*, p. 112)

G. Fohrer, *Introduction to the Old Testament* (London: SPCK, 1970) (ET of *Einleitung in das Alte Testament* [Heidelberg: Quelle & Meyer, 1965]), pp. 419-21.

A German scholar has written an informative account of the pre-critical interpretation of Hosea 1–3:

S. Bitter, *Die Ehe des Propheten Hosea. Eine auslegungs-geschichtliche Untersuchung* (Göttingen: Vandenhoeck & Ruprecht, 1975).

Rudolph's views on the problem are contained in his commentary on Hosea, pp. 39-49, 86-90. A favourable account of them in English can be found in R.E. Clements's article cited at the end of Chapter 2. Other recent studies of Hosea's marriage include:

A. Deissler, 'Die Interpretation von Hos 1,2-9 in den Hosea-Kommentaren von H.W. Wolff und W. Rudolph im kritischen Vergleich', in J. Schreiner (ed.), *Wort, Lied und Gottesspruch* (Festschrift for J. Ziegler; Würzburg: Echter, 1972), II, pp. 129-36.

J. Schreiner, 'Hoseas Ehe, ein Zeichen des Gerichts', *BZ* ns 21 (1977), pp. 163-83.

M.J. Geller, 'The Elephantine Papyri and Hosea 2,3', *JSJ* 8 (1977), pp. 139-48.

7

LITERARY CRITICISM AND
THE BOOK OF HOSEA

THE TERM 'LITERARY CRITICISM' has been deliberately
chosen for the title of this chapter because of its ambiguity in
present-day biblical studies. On the one hand, it has been
used as a general term for those methods of critical study
which have dominated Old Testament scholarship for most of
the past hundred years and more: source criticism, form
criticism, tradition criticism and redaction criticism. These are
methods with a sharply historical and analytical emphasis,
although they have always been based on a careful study of
the complete text of the Bible. On the other hand, and
especially in the past twenty years, 'literary criticism' has
come to mean in biblical studies the same kind or kinds of
study that are called by this name in the wider world of the
appreciation of literature, whether English, French, classical
or any other. In such study the emphasis falls much more on
the literary product itself than on the process by which it was
created and attention is devoted above all to its meaning and
its artistic qualities and techniques. Of course literary criticism
in this sense covers a very broad spectrum of approaches and
some of these are (or have been) closer to, and others further
away from, the other kind of literary criticism in biblical studies.

The growing interest in such approaches among biblical
scholars has undoubtedly helped to draw attention to features
of the Old Testament which had tended to be neglected, but it
has also led, perhaps inevitably, to the adoption of extreme
positions as some scholars have seemed to want to replace the
older, historically-oriented methods of study altogether with

the new ones, while on the other side the newer approaches have been entirely rejected or disregarded by those who thought them unduly subjective or governed by a predisposition to find particular patterns or 'structures' in the texts. This is not the place to deal in detail with the general theoretical issues involved, but I hope that the juxtaposition of the two sections of this chapter will help to underline my confidence that both kinds of approach, used judiciously, have a important part to play in assisting our appreciation and evaluation of the book of Hosea.

Source Criticism

Source criticism of the prophetic books has traditionally been mainly concerned with distinguishing between 'authentic' utterances or compositions of the prophet after whom a particular book is named and 'secondary additions', often from a much later period. Some attention has also been given to identifying the major sections of which a book is composed and to defining where one poem ends and the next begins. We shall focus our attention here on the question of 'authenticity'. As often happens, it is to one of the older commentaries that one must look to find a full account of the reasons why scholars came to the conclusion that certain passages in Hosea could not have been spoken by the prophet himself. The commentary of W.R. Harper on Amos and Hosea, published in 1905 in the *International Critical Commentary* series, is a good and widely available example of this: see pp. clviii-clxiii for his general discussion of the subject, and the comments on individual passages for specific arguments. Harper divides the passages which he believes to be 'secondary' (i.e. not by Hosea) into five categories:

1. most of the references to Judah;
2. 'the so-called Messianic allusions', that is passages which speak of the restoration and future prosperity of Israel in their homeland;
3. passages, mainly short, 'of a technical, archaeological or historical character', which were designed to expand or explain an original saying;

4. miscellaneous glosses and interpolations for which no particular reason can be discerned;
5. the concluding comment in 14.9.

Harper gives several kinds of reason for denying a Hosean origin to a passage: often more than one is cited in a particular case. References to Judah were in most cases, he believed, beside the point for Hosea himself, who was speaking to the northern kingdom, but it is readily understandable that a later Judaean editor would want to ensure that his own people were mentioned. If a phrase appeared which belonged to a later stage of the language, or if the regular poetic metre was disturbed, this would be an additional sign that unoriginal elements were present. Of course this kind of argument presupposed detailed study of the Hebrew language and of metrical patterns on the part of the commentator, and Harper and his contemporaries paid much more attention to such matters than most recent commentaries have done. Another kind of argument used was inconsistency. In dealing with the passages in group (2), Harper contrasted them with the imminent and inexorable doom of which Hosea spoke elsewhere: 'These passages, therefore, are deemed entirely inconsistent with Hosea's point of view, directly contradicting the representations which are fundamental in his preaching.' Again, a passage might express ideas which are characteristic of a later phase of Israelite prophecy. In some cases, finally, a verse or verses seemed to interrupt the logical development of the thought: if these were removed, the original sequence could be clearly seen. In a particular case, of course, an argument belonging to none of these types might be used, such as one based on the unsuitability of a phrase to its immediate context.

Arguments of these general kinds have continued to be used for the identification of later elements in Hosea and the books of other prophets, but not always with the same results. In particular, further research has suggested that arguments from metrical structure and the history of the Hebrew language very often assume a rigidity about these phenomena which is both improbable and unproven. Harper and the commentators of his time were probably unduly confident in their ability to recognize individual words that had been

added to Hosea's oracles. A similar criticism can be made of a
more recent tendency to label phrases as 'Deuteronomistic'
and therefore secondary. An important example of this is
L. Perlitt's denial that the reference to 'covenant' in 8.1 is from
Hosea himself, chiefly on the ground that parallels to the
expressions used are found in Deuteronomy and related
books. In one particular area these conclusions have been
widely challenged, though not entirely abandoned. This
concerns the oracles of future hope (group [2] above). Nearly
all recent commentaries on Hosea (Jeremias is an exception)
have treated them as genuine words of the prophet, with the
exception sometimes of 1.10–2.1 and one or two other verses.
This is partly because scholars are more prepared than they
were to accept that a prophet like Hosea who was active over
a long period in a deteriorating political situation (see Chapter
1) might well have spoken differently at one time from
another. The very relatedness of prophecy to its original
historical context, which is one of the major fresh developments of modern Old Testament study, would lead us to
expect this. And it is with a 'different' message rather than an
'inconsistent' one, to use Harper's word, that we are often
dealing, for the point of the salvation oracles is not that
judgment will be avoided but that after it, and even because
of it, there is hope. The other reason for a changed view of the
authenticity of these passages is that closer study of them has
revealed that there is a clear continuity of themes and concerns between them and the judgment oracles. This is particularly clear in Hosea 11, where it is precisely the patient and
caring love of God which Israel has despised (vv. 1-4) that
cannot in the end remain content with an outcome which
involves the annihilation of the beloved (vv. 8-9).

Form Criticism

Form criticism was introduced to Old Testament scholarship
by Hermann Günkel at the beginning of the twentieth century. It was intended to be a central feature of the history of
biblical literature which it was his (never wholly fulfilled)
ambition to write. Günkel began from the insight that in early

times literature was tightly bound by conventional rules which prescribed the formal and other characteristics which were appropriate for utterances in particular recurring situations in the life of a society. In the course of time these rules might be modified or abandoned altogether, and forms of speech designed for one situation (*Sitz im Leben*) might be transferred to another. It was the task of the historian of biblical literature to identify the different types (*Gattungen*: sing. *Gattung*) of composition which were present in a particular text, to describe their characteristic features and to indicate their relation to similar texts elsewhere.

According to C. Westermann the classic *Gattung* of prophetic speech was the announcement of judgment, which appeared first as an utterance directed against a single individual and later against the nation of Israel (or Judah) as a whole. This speech-form comprised two main parts, the announcement of judgment in the strict sense and an accusation which provided the rationale for the coming judgment. The connection between these two elements, which earlier scholars had often treated quite separately, was made by a transitional particle such as 'Therefore' or 'Because', which was often linked with the formula 'Thus says the Lord'. This formula Westermann called the 'messenger-formula', because its structure was the same as that used to introduce messages and letters from one human being to another (e.g. Gen. 45.9). It provided an appropriate introduction to the characteristic prophetic mode of speech in which Yahweh himself was presented as the speaker in the first person singular.

While this pattern of analysis works quite well in many of the prophetic books, it proves to be quite unsuited as it stands to the book of Hosea. The messenger-formula itself never appears (though divine speech itself is very common) and most of the individual sections do not conform closely to the pattern of the announcement of judgment described above or to any other pattern (2.5-13 and 4.1-3 do fit to some extent). More often elements of announcement and accusation are woven together in a more complex composition, including elements of other kinds as well. For example, 9.1-9 begins with a warning (v. 1a), which leads into an accusation (v. 1b)

and an announcement of judgment (vv. 2-7a) which is inter-
rupted by a mocking question (v. 5). Verses 7b-9 appear to
represent a disputation between the prophet and his audience, and conclude with a fresh accusation and announcement of judgment (v. 9).

Westermann was well aware that not all prophetic speech
corresponded to his 'classic pattern', and he identified several
variants of it and of associated speech-forms. Moreover, he
recognized that in later Old Testament prophecy the
announcement of judgment practically disappeared. He seems,
however, not to have taken sufficient account of the fact that
in Hosea, who is one of the earliest of the prophets whose
oracles survive in any number, the 'classic pattern' has
already largely lost its sharp outlines. This may well be a
mark of the literary independence and sophistication of
Hosea, of which more will be said later. But whatever its
cause, it suggests that a form-critical approach to Hosea will
have to content itself with identifying recurring features of
his oracles, without necessarily being able to give to whole
passages descriptions which group them conveniently into a
small number of categories. The example of 9.1-9 is an indication that elements of accusation and announcement of
judgment certainly appear in Hosea, and in fact large sections
of his sayings can be classified in these terms. But those who
have worked through the whole text of Hosea have detected
elements of many other types as well.

To begin with, there are the two narrative sections in chs. 1
and 3, the former in the third person ('biographical'), the latter in the first person ('autobiographical') style. Both, however, belong from the point of view of their content to the
category of descriptions of a prophetic symbolic action. These
typically begin with a divine command (1.2 [cf. vv. 4, 6, 9];
3.1) and in the full form (as here) continue with an account of
the prophet's performance of the symbolic action(s). The
emphasis falls not on the biographical aspect as such but on
the divine initiative and on the message which is embodied in
the symbolic action. This is of course the reason why these
narratives are so ill-suited to the answering of the precise
biographical questions which scholars have often brought to

them (see Chapter 6). In fact their main elements correspond closely to those of certain of Hosea's oracles; for example 1.2-9 contains elements of accusation (v. 2; cf. v. 4) and announcement of judgment (vv. 4-5, 6, 9).

In dealing with the poetic oracles themselves it will be necessary to be brief and to refer to the commentaries (in English especially that by H.W. Wolff) for a fuller account. A feature which is particularly characteristic of Hosea is the historical retrospect, within which we may distinguish the rehearsing of Yahweh's saving acts on behalf of his people (e.g. 9.10a; 11.1-4; 12.13; 13.4-6) from the citation of Israel's ancient sins (e.g. 2.5; 9.10b; 10.1; 12.2-4). Two of the oracles are introduced by the term 'indictment' (4.1; 12.2: Heb. *rib*), which has strong legal connotations. Then there are exhortations in the imperative mood, some of them simply calling attention to what is to follow (4.1; 5.1), others commending or warning against actions of a particular kind (e.g. 4.15b; 9.1; 10.12; 12.6; 14.1-3). Related to these are the 'call to penitence' in 6.1-3 and the 'divine instruction' in 6.6:

For I desire steadfast love and not sacrifice,
the knowledge of God rather than burnt offerings.

The examples of exhortations cited above all speak about God in the third person. Wolff and others call this non-representative style 'prophetic speech' to emphasize that the prophet here speaks in his own right rather than as the messenger of God, but it might be clearer to use the expression 'non-oracular' for such passages. The same style appears elsewhere, for example in proverbial sayings (4.11, 14b; 8.7; 14.9) and in prophetic reactions at the end of an oracle or stanza (e.g. 4.16; 9.14, 17; 13.15-16). Finally there are the salvation oracles. Although these are characterized chiefly by the content, certain typical formulae also appear: thus 'On that day' in 2.16, 2.18 and 2.21 and 'in the latter days' in 3.5. The structure of these oracles varies considerably (in Hosea this is no surprise!), but it is interesting to note that, while the dominant verb forms are first-person statements about the future referring to Yahweh's action, these several times lead into third-person statements about Israel's subsequent response (2.15, 20, 23; 11.11). This both resembles and is distinct from the typical judgment speech, where the combination of Israel's action and Yahweh's action also appears, but in which Israel's wrongdoing (commonly referred to in the past tense) precedes and is the reason for the coming divine judgment. Another common feature of the salvation oracles is the reversal of an earlier announcement of judgment: this is particularly clear in the treatment of the names of Hosea's children in 2.22-23 (compare also 11.11 with 11.5, and 14.4 with 9.15).

Form criticism has traditionally concerned itself not only with the conventional and formulaic aspects of literature but with the origins of the *Gattungen* in particular kinds of situations (*Sitz im Leben*). Some of the features mentioned above can be correlated with typical elements in a prophet's situation, for example the exhortations, which presuppose a public and perhaps a hostile context for his speaking. In other cases Hosea seems to be using forms of speech which derive from occasions that were not specifically prophetic. The 'wisdom' sayings would be one example, though the precise context of their use remains elusive. The indictment sayings probably owe something to a judicial background, but it is not clear how much. The same should probably be said of the accusations of Israel under the guise of an unfaithful wife (2.2-13) and a rebellious son (11.1-7). We know that such matters were the subject of proceedings which could lead to the death penalty (cf. Deut. 21.18-21; 22.22), but our evidence of what was said on such occasions is very limited and insufficient for us to judge how closely Hosea was following a standard pattern. Wolff's suggestion that the exhortations, especially 2.2-4, are based on a legal 'proposal to reach a settlement' (*Schlichtungsvorschlag*) again suffers from the lack of genuinely judicial examples. A more solid foundation perhaps exists for the view that some passages are modelled on cultic prototypes: the 'call to penitence' in 6.1-3 (compare Ps. 122.1; Lam. 3.40-42), the recitation of Yahweh's saving acts in, for example, 11.1-4 (cf. Ps. 80.8-11), the 'divine self-introduction formulae' in 12.9 and 13.4 (cf. Ps. 50.7; 81.10). All this is, however, a long way from proving the view once held (e.g. by A. Weiser) that practically every saying in the book could be related to some feature of the annual covenant-renewal festival of Yahweh!

Tradition Criticism

Tradition criticism (or tradition history, as it is sometimes called) has been applied to two different aspects of the prophetic books. One of these, the relationship of prophecy to older traditions such as the exodus or the law, has already been extensively treated in relation to Hosea in Chapter 5. The other focus of this kind of study is the transmission of the oracles of a prophet through subsequent generations. This, too, does not need extensive treatment here because it overlaps to a large extent with the subject of the next section, redaction criticism. Where the two terms are distinguished, tradition criticism tends to be concerned with an oral stage in the collection and transmission of prophetic sayings, during which there is still a direct link (for example through a circle or succession of disciples) with the prophet.

Opinions have varied among scholars about the length of time to be assigned to the oral stage of the tradition (if indeed there was such a stage, which some have doubted). Some scholars, especially in Scandinavia, in conformity with their general emphasis on the importance of oral tradition in the formation of the Old Testament, have supposed it to have continued for a century or more, before the oracles were written down. This, on the one hand, assumes extensive memorizing by a circle of 'tradents', but also (for this to serve a worthwhile purpose) a continuing use of the oracles in community life and probably some elaboration of them as the prophet's ideas were developed in new oracles and in interpretations of old ones. The association of oracles by means of 'catchwords' (e.g. 'devour' in 8.7 and 'swallowed up' on 8.8, which are the same verb in the Hebrew), which could be devices to aid memorization, might be a sign that the collection existed at first in an oral form. Yet such features are quite rare in Hosea, as in the other prophetic books, and the hypothesis of a long period of oral transmission remains at best unproven.

The majority view now is that written collections of the prophets' sayings were made early (already 'during the prophet's lifetime' according to Wolff, p. xxxi), even if a parallel oral tradition also existed. Such oral collections could, for example, have also preserved additional oracles composed by Hosea's disciples and modifications to his sayings (such as, perhaps, 2.17; 4.1a; 6.1-3; 10.12-13a, 15) until there was a need to make a fresh written copy. This means that, while the production of material additional to Hosea's own words should probably be traced to some kind of setting in which they were being recited and discussed, there was from the beginning a literary (i.e. written) aspect to their collection and amplification. That brings us to a consideration of redaction criticism, or the study of the editing of the book, the most recently developed of the critical methods described here, and one which is the focus of much current interest (see further the bibliography).

Redaction Criticism

To a large extent redaction criticism can be viewed as source criticism in reverse. Source criticism seeks to 'peel off' the later additions so as to bring us as close as possible to a prophet's own words; redaction criticism picks up the 'peelings', as it were, and investigates what they can tell us about the motives, methods and circumstances of those who made these additions to the original text. It follows that redaction criticism begins by being dependent on the findings of source criticism. But it also brings a much more positive evaluation to the so-called 'secondary' material, and treats it with the same seriousness as the original sayings of the prophet. These later voices, too, are part of the prophetic tradition of Israel, and without them we should probably not have had the prophetic books at all.

Before considering the addition of new material to the collection of Hosea's sayings, we should remember that those sayings themselves had to be selected and put together. Reference has already been made in an earlier chapter of this book to the special focus of chs. 1–3 on the prophet's 'marriage' and the use of marital imagery for Yahweh's relationship to Israel. Here material of diverse character and origin has been brought together under a common theme into what could at one time have been a separate Hosean collection. The short sayings which comprise the nucleus of chs. 4–14 are much less consistent in their overall theme, but it is noticeable that 'blocks' within these chapters do show some continuity of subject matter. For example, 4.1-3 are a general 'indictment' against the whole land for wrongdoing, whose cause is then traced from v. 4 onwards to the failings of the priesthood and the people's religious misdemeanours ('whoredom'). 5.1-7, though apparently a separate unit with a fresh introduction, continues the same themes. 5.8–7.16, on the other hand, deal mainly with political matters, initially war and relations with foreign peoples (5.8-14), then internal problems (6.7–7.7) and finally foreign relations again (7.8-16). Wolff argued that these 'kerygmatic units' were the record of particular appearances of the prophet (*Auftrittsskizzen*), the later sayings often being his responses to objections raised by his audience which the tradition did not preserve (except in 9.7 and perhaps in 4.4a). Thus he conjectured that after 4.6 the priest initially addressed may have defended himself by referring to the practice of other priests throughout the land, while following 4.15 he thinks that the people may have affirmed their confidence in the sanctuaries, perhaps by quoting a text like Ps. 23.1 (cf. v. 16b). This is an interesting theory, with some support in the text, and if it is correct it presents us with some very vivid evidence of the cut-and-thrust of a prophet in debate with his audience. But the facts which it is designed to explain can just as well be explained by envisaging a process whereby utterances on similar subjects were strung together as a convenient way of giving some order to the collections. Chronological considerations also seem to have played some part, but that need not mean that adjacent passages were juxtaposed because they were known to derive from the very same occasion.

A little more should be said about the way that chs. 4–14 as a whole have been arranged. As they stand they exhibit a repeated sequence of announcements of judgment followed by oracles of restoration:

	A	B
Judgment	4.1–10.15	11.12–13.16
Restoration	11.1-11	14.1-9

This repeats a pattern that can be found in ch. 1 and in chs. 2–3, as well as, for example, in Amos. Here the repetition of the pattern is probably due to the combination of what were once two separate collections of Hosea's sayings. It is also striking that close to the beginning of both sections there is a reference to the 'indictment' which Yahweh has against his people (4.1; 12.2). Further support for such a view has been seen in the concluding formula 'says the Lord' (11.11), which is not found otherwise in Hosea outside chs. 1–2. That may, however, be a concluding formula only to the oracle in ch. 11 itself (cf. 2.13). Presumably, if this view is correct, any original introduction to chs. 12–14 was omitted when the two collections of sayings were joined together. It is not only in their overall structure that chs. 4–11 and 12–14 are parallel: many of the same themes recur in both. One interesting difference between them is the total absence of the metaphor of 'whoredom' from chs. 12–14 (contrast ch. 4 *passim*; 5.3-4; 6.10; 8.9-10; 9.1).

A number of possible additions to the oracles of Hosea have already been mentioned in connection with tradition criticism. It is impossible to pin down the time or the place of their origin with any precision, except that they probably originated in a period after the fall of Samaria to the Assyrians, when Hosea's announcements of judgment on the northern kingdom were dramatically fulfilled. Some other additions to the original collections can be related more specifically to historical circumstances and provide an interesting commentary on their subsequent use and interpretation. The first of these is 1.7, which states that Yahweh is to make a discrimination between the kingdoms of Israel and Judah: Israel, the northern kingdom, will be cast off, but Judah will experience Yahweh's salvation in a deliverance in which military might will play no part. The strong pro-Judaean theology (compare Ps. 78.67–72) argues for an origin after Hosea's oracles had been brought to Judah, and the specific character of the hope associates the saying closely with the portrayal of Sennacherib's attack on Jerusalem in Isaiah and in 2 Kings 18–19. A number of other references to Judah in Hosea seem to be redactional, but to derive from a different milieu, closer to that of Judaean prophets of judgment such as Jeremiah. A clear instance is 12.2:

> The Lord has an indictment against Judah,
> and will punish Jacob according to his ways.

Since the following verse plays on the names of Jacob and *Israel* (see the commentaries), the first name must originally have been 'Israel'; and the change to 'Judah' reflects an intention to bring Judah under the same condemnation as that which Hosea had previously pronounced against Israel and indeed to highlight this. In 6.11a the 'also' suggests an afterthought, threatening doom on Judah as well as Israel. Two further verses which mention Judah, each rather isolated from its context, have close similarities to verses in Amos:

> Though you play the whore, O Israel,
>   do not let Judah become guilty.
> Do not enter into Gilgal,
>   or go up to Beth-aven,
> and do not swear 'As the Lord lives' (4.15; cf. Amos. 5.4-6; 8.14).

> Israel has forgotten his Maker
>   and built palaces;
> and Judah has multiplied fortified cities;
> but I will send a fire upon his cities,
> and it shall devour his strongholds (8.14; cf. Amos 1.4 etc.).

The evidence suggests that here oracles addressed to Judah were added to the Hosea tradition by people who knew and revered the sayings of Amos, which had also originally been addressed to the northern kingdom and which also underwent a 'Judaean redaction' (see especially Amos 2.4-5). We have here a first sign, perhaps, of a growing corpus ('canon'?) of prophetic literature which was being adapted to new situations by people who saw themselves as disciples of more than a single prophet.

While these changes may antedate the fall of Jerusalem to the Babylonians in 587/86 BCE, it is probable that the last line of 5.5 was added after that catastrophe, as its verb is most naturally translated in the past tense, in contrast to those of the preceding lines:

> Judah also *has stumbled* with them.

A very similar addition has been detected in 4.5, 'the prophet also shall stumble with you by night'—a notion which is both alien to Hosea's other statements about prophets and very much in line with the criticism of prophets which we find in a passage such as Jeremiah 23.

Further additions to the book were designed to enrich its hopes for the future restoration of Israel by the insertion of themes that were prominent in the Babylonian exile and afterwards. 1.10–2.1 carry further the reversal of the names of Hosea's children, begun in 2.22-23, with prophecies of a great increase of population and the reunion of the divided kingdoms under a single ruler; 2.18 speaks of harmony with the animal world and an end to war; the addition of 'and David their king' in 3.5 gives a specific political character to Israel's restoration; and, on the most probable interpretation, 11.10 associates a return of the exiles with Yahweh's judgment on the Gentile nations (cf. Joel 3.16). Parallels to the ideas expressed in these additions can be found in a variety of late prophetic texts, as threats of judgment on Israel gave way to a predominantly positive eschatology. All of them recur, for example, in Ezekiel 34–39. The language used suggests a knowledge on the part of the redactors of a wide range of prophetic and other literature; this confirms a growing scholarly tendency to detect the 'interpretation of Scripture by Scripture', as our prophetic canon and Old Testament took shape in exilic and postexilic times. One striking omission deserves to be mentioned: no attempt was made to introduce into Hosea the temple ('Zion') theology of Jerusalem which occupies such a prominent place particularly in later prophecy (see, e.g. Joel 3.16, cited above). Was this, perhaps, because it continued to be recognized that, as a northerner, Hosea stood outside the Jerusalem tradition? Or were his polemics against the other ancient shrines, such as Bethel and Gilgal, thought to be sufficient to vindicate, by implication, the sole legitimacy of Jerusalem?

The book of Hosea as we have it is furnished with introductory and concluding verses which were designed to guide its interpretation. In the introduction the emphasis falls on historical context and divine origin. It is notable that the kings of

Judah are placed first in 1.1, which suggests a Judaean origin for this verse: its form most closely resembles the introductory verses of Micah and Zephaniah, both Judaean prophets, and the list of Judaean kings actually makes Hosea an exact contemporary of Isaiah, which may be deliberate. Traces of an older heading to the book, which also lays stress on its divine origin, have been detected at the beginning of 1.2, which can be translated:

> (This is) the beginning of the Lord's speaking through Hosea.
> (cf. NEB, REB)

The concluding verse of the book (14.9) is a unique feature, although Ps. 107.42-43 is somewhat similar. It is a kind of postscript which draws out the lasting value of this collection of oracles. Interestingly this is seen to lie not in a preview of future history but in the confirmation that God's ways are right and disobedience brings disaster (the word 'stumble' is a favourite of Hosea's: see 4.5, 5.5, 14.1). John Barton has written of such an understanding of prophecy:

> There is probably no book in the Latter Prophets that lacks some evidence of this desire of the redactors to show the ethical relevance of older prophecy and history to contemporary ethical needs (*Oracles of God*, p.158).

Although he does not mention it specifically, there could be no better illustration of this than Hosea 14.9.

The Poetry of Hosea

One of the best reasons for learning Hebrew is that this allows a far greater appreciation of the qualities of Hebrew poetry. To a certain extent, where the content is concerned, these qualities come through clearly enough in translation, but much that is based on the actual sound and rhythm of the Hebrew words is difficult if not impossible to reproduce. In a guide which is designed chiefly for those who read the Old Testament in English some of these stylistic features can only be made intelligible by giving an English translation which will at times seem rather stilted, because the Hebrew word-order is being closely followed, and in some cases by adding the original Hebrew in transliterated form.

Parallelism
We may begin with some simple examples of the verse-forms which Hosea uses:

(a) What shall I do with you, O Ephraim? What shall I do with you, O Judah? (6.4a)

(b) But shall-return Ephraim to Egypt, and in Assyria unclean (food) they shall eat (9.3b; NRSV modified)

(c) For steadfast love I desire and not sacrifice, and knowledge of God rather than burnt-offerings (6.6; NRSV modified)

(d) Blow the-horn in-Gibeah, the-trumpet in-Ramah! *tiqʻu šopar baggibʻah /hᵃṣoṣᵉrah bᵉramah* (5.8a)

It has been well-known since the work of Robert Lowth in the eighteenth century that Hebrew poetry (like other Semitic poetry) frequently exhibits parallelism or repetition of thought in the two parts of a standard poetic line. Exact parallelism, as in (a) above, is comparatively rare in prophecy, and this is a particularly unusual case in that the very same words occupy two-thirds of each half-line (also known as a 'colon', plural 'cola'). More often parallelism occurs, as in (b), with a change of order in the matching components, which may produce a chiastic effect (here: verb...place-name; place-name...verb). A further variation in this instance is the omission of the subject ('Ephraim') in the second half-line, where an object ('unclean food') is required by the transitive verb 'eat', to keep the two half-lines equal in length. (c) is another example of incomplete parallelism, this time without any change of order in the component parts: the verb 'I desire' is not repeated or matched in the second half-line, but the latter maintains the balance of length by the use of a two-word object, 'knowledge of God', to correspond to 'steadfast love', which is a single word (*ḥesed*) in the Hebrew. Sometimes the balance between the two half-lines is not maintained, one being shorter than the other, as in (d). This line-form (3 + 2 stressed elements) raises an interesting question, because it is the rhythm favoured in the lament for the dead (Heb. *qinah*): e.g. Lamentations *passim*, and a clear prophetic example in Amos 5.2. Does its use in Hosea (for other examples see, e.g., 7.1b, 10.8aα, 11.12) indicate a 'funerary' character for his message, for which ch. 13 might provide some explicit support? The answer is probably 'no', because the 3 + 2 line is by no means limited to funerary laments: compare, for example, 1 Sam. 18.7 and Song 1.10.

Three-part lines (tricola) are also found, both with parallelism and as a form of list. In this case the cola are often shorter than they are in two-part lines (bicola):

(e) Stricken is Ephraim, their root is dried up, fruit they-shall-not-bear (NRSV modified).
hukkah 'eprayim / šoršam yabeš / p^eri bal-ya^{'a}śun (9.16a)

(f) With the beasts of the field, and with the birds of the air, and even the fish of the sea shall perish (NRSV modified).
b^ehayat haśśadeh / ub^{e'}op haššamayim / w^egam d^ege hayyam ye'asepu (4.3b).

Hosea also packs a list of three items into a single half-line several times:

(g) Under oak and poplar and terebinth, because their shade is good (4.13aβ NRSV modified).

Compare 2.10, 4.2 and 9.11.

Figures of Speech
Coming to some examples of figures of speech, we may note first how Hosea likes to use similarities of sound, both for ornament and to express indignation and irony:

(h) Surely like a heifer stubborn, stubborn is Israel (NRSV modified)
ki k^eparah sorerah / sarar yiśra'el (4.16a).

(i) A wild ass (*pere'*) wandering alone; Ephraim (*'eprayim*) has bargained for lovers (8.9b).

(j) Egypt shall gather them (*t^eqabb^esem*), Memphis shall bury them (*t^eqabb^erem*) (9.6a).

(h) illustrates alliteration (k, r and the sibilants), assonance (the a-vowels), repetition of etymologically related words and possibly paronomasia (word-play): note the echo of *sarar* in *yiśra'el*. Paronomasia is particularly common over the name 'Ephraim': see example (e) above (*'eprayim...p^eri*) and now (i), where *pere'* ('wild ass') is presented as a pseudo-etymology of the name. Even rhyme, which is very rare in Hebrew poetry, is found several times in Hosea, as in (j).

Hosea has a particular propensity for certain words, such as 'commit whoredom' (Heb. *zanah*) and its derivatives (1.2 etc.), 'return' (*šub*) in various senses, and the adverb 'now' (*'attah*). 'Now' is used in two distinct ways. Sometimes it appears in accusations, often at the climax, implying 'after everything else, *now* this!' (e.g. 5.3); elsewhere it expresses the imminence of judgment (e.g. 5.7). Another aspect of Hosea's vocabulary is his frequent use of geographical names, both in sequences (5.1, 8) and to allude to famous episodes of history (e.g. 9.9, 10, 15).

Imagery
Imagery is widely used to achieve greater vividness: it is more frequent in Hosea then any other prophet. Similes are particularly common, both to represent Israel (as in example [h] above) and to characterize Yahweh's action. An example of the latter which also illustrates the pairing of similes which Hebrew parallelism encourages is 5.12:

(k) Therefore I am *like maggots* to Ephraim, and *like rottenness* to the house of Judah.

Whole series of similes are found in 13.7-8 and 14.5-7, portraying doom in the first case and renewal in the second. A single simile may be developed over several lines, as with the baking oven in 7.4-7. Hosea also freely uses metaphor, both in individual phrases (as in example [e] above and in 13.12) and in longer sustained narratives. The two classic examples of the latter are the representation of Israel as Yahweh's unfaithful wife in 2.2-15 (together with the 'new marriage' language in vv. 16, 19 and 20) and the portrayal of Israel as a beloved but disobedient child in 11.1-4. In the latter passage it has been common to say that Yahweh is represented as the father of Israel, but recently Marie-Theres Wacker has very properly pointed out that the actions described in vv. 3 and 4 are just as characteristic of a mother as of a father, if not more so. There is also an important shift here from sexuality to parenthood as a figure for the love of Yahweh.

Negation
One final aspect of Hosea's poetic language may be noted: the prominence of negation, both implicit and explicit. Whereas Amos was adept at giving an ironic twist to familiar religious language (e.g. 'rescue' in Amos 3.12 and apparently 'the day of the Lord' in 5.18-20), Hosea prefers the more direct negative, or at least an expression equivalent to a negative. This appears already in the names given to two of his children in 1.6 and 1.9 (cf. 2.4) and in the blunt statement in 2.2: 'she is not my wife, and I am not her husband'. In 4.16 the implied answer to the question about the traditional image of the divine shepherd must be a clear 'No':

(1) Can the Lord now feed them like a lamb in a broad pasture?

There is no knowledge (4.6; 5.4) and no repentance (5.4; 7.10; 11.5), and two longer sequences of negatives appear in 3.4 and 4.1 (in both cases the repeated Hebrew word is *'en*, 'there is not/shall not be'). Israel will not find Yahweh (5.6; cf. 9.12), he will not love them any more (9.15). There is rejection, not acceptance, for both priest (4.6) and people (9.17). Further examples could be given. Of course this is not the only way in which Hosea speaks about sin and judgment, but it is prominent enough to deserve special mention.

Why Did Hosea Write in Poetry?

We turn, finally, from these poetic features to a brief consideration of the more general question of their function within Hosea's oracles. Robert Alter has raised the question, why did the Hebrew prophets cast their urgent messages in verse? He notes that prose is found in the prophetic books particularly in

passages where the prophet's commissioning by God is
described (as in Hos. 1 and 3), but that the oracles of the
prophets themselves tend to be cast in verse, which has a
peculiarly 'vocative' character: that is, it is 'a form of direct
address to a historically real audience'. But why in verse? Is it
simply to make what is said more forceful and more memorable? Alter thinks not, and makes the very interesting alternative suggestion that the use of the poetic form is appropriate because prophetic speech is typically 'represented speech',
in the sense that the prophet's human words represent the
words of God to his people. This fits in, as he says, with the
common prophetic usage of various introductory and concluding formulae and of the 'divine first person pronoun', as well
with the call narratives which appear in certain prophetic
books. It also fits in well with the notion of all poetic language
as 'fictive' (Barbara Hernstein Smith) rather than natural.
Perhaps the use of the poetic form in ancient and classical
English drama is also illuminating here, both in the representative character of such a performance and in the seriousness
of the issues treated and the formality of the occasion.

In the particular instance of Hosea at least two further
factors can be seen to have played an important part in his
choice, or at least his use, of the poetic medium. One is his
deployment of the most varied and evocative imagery, which
has already been mentioned. It is not necessary, and probably
not correct, to introduce here the idea of archetypal images, as
Alter does. It is true that a popular line of interpretation has
suggested that Hosea took over the imagery of marriage
ready-made from the fertility cult and gave it a new and anti-
thetical formulation. But it is far from clear, for example, that
the fertility cult of the Levant in Hosea's time knew anything
of a 'sacred marriage' between a god and the earth. Of course
marriage subsequently *became* an archetypal image in biblical
literature of a later period, but that is another issue. A better
case could be made for seeing the vine of Hos. 10.1 as such an
archetypal image (cf. Ps. 80). But as we have seen, most of the
images which Hosea uses and elaborates in a variety of ways
are more closely related to his very specific warnings to his
contemporaries than to generalized abstractions about the

way the world is. Although he uses some traditional material, Hosea is in this respect as in others standing at the beginning of a new phase of biblical literature, in which the primary task of his imagery is to evoke as powerfully as possible the startlingly new states of affairs which he perceives in the relationship between Yahweh and Israel. So like Amos he seizes on the image of the lion for Yahweh and enriches it with references to other wild animals (5.14; 13.7-8) and to 'devouring' (5.7; 7.7, 9; 11.6), and he creates the picture of the enraged divine husband who threatens and then exposes his unfaithful wife (ch. 2). Equally, when a dramatic restoration is to be spoken of, he will turn to images of healing, fertility and the migration of birds (6.1-3; 11.11; 14.4-8).

The second factor in Hosea's use of the poetic form is its ability to express pathos. W.R. Harper commented long ago that, when compared with Amos, the rhythm of Hosea's poetry is 'inferior...there being many passages where the movement is halting and broken'. We may doubt whether this value-judgment is appropriate to what is in itself a perceptive observation. The very fluctuation in the rhythmical patterns of Hosea's poetry, the departure from the more regular measure of cult poetry, created a highly effective medium for the expression of the emotional upheaval appropriate to a prophet who knew that he had to speak unheard of things about Yahweh and Israel. Even when he came to speak, at first haltingly (11.8-9), of the possibility of a new beginning, he could only do this with fear and trembling. The same effect was achieved by another favourite device of the prophet, also noted by Harper: asyndeton. The abrupt placing together of short clauses, sometimes several in succession, without any connecting particle, is used to paint a picture of the people's many-sided rebellion against Yahweh (cf. 4.18; 10.1) or to indicate the relentless blows of the coming doom:

> For behold—they have escaped destruction,
>> Egypt shall gather them, Memphis shall bury them,
>> nettles shall possess their precious things of silver,
>> thorns shall be in their tents.
> The days of punishment have come,
>> the days of recompense have come, Israel shall know (9.6-7a,
> NRSV modified).

Compare also example (e) above.

Hosea's prophecy became a pattern for Judaean writers of a hundred years later and more. If this is largely due to his ability to plumb the depths of divine judgement without losing hold of God's love, it is nevertheless also likely that it was his use of the poetic form, which we have only begun to appreciate, that ensured that this thought had the fullest possible impact.

Further Reading

A very balanced literary treatment of the twelve 'minor' prophets is given by H. Marks in the *The Literary Guide to the Bible* (ed. R. Alter and F. Kermode; London: Collins, 1987), pp. 207-33.

A useful summary of early form-critical work on the prophetic books can be found at the beginning of C. Westermann's *Basic Forms of Prophetic Speech* (London: Lutterworth Press, 1967), which is itself an important general contribution to the subject (see also his *Prophetic Oracles of Salvation in the Old Testament* [Philadelphia: Westminster Press, 1991]).

The recent popularity of a redaction-critical approach to the prophets can be seen in Jörg Jeremias's commentary (above, p. 12) and in:
G.I. Emmerson, *Hosea. An Israelite Prophet in Judaean Perspective* (JSOTSup, 28; Sheffield: JSOT Press, 1984).
G.A. Yee, *Composition and Tradition in the Book of Hosea. A Redaction-Critical Investigation* (SBLDS, 102; Atlanta: Scholars Press, 1987).

See also:
J. Barton, *Oracles of God: Perceptions of Ancient Prophecy in Israel after the Exile* (London: Darton, Longman & Todd, 1986).

For an appreciation of the literary features of Hosea reference may be made to:
W.G.E. Watson, *Classical Hebrew Poetry. A Guide to its Techniques* (JSOTSup, 26; Sheffield: JSOT Press, 1984).
R. Alter, *The Art of Biblical Poetry* (New York: Basic Books, 1985), ch. 6.
M.-T. Wacker, 'God as Mother? On the Meaning of a Biblical God-Symbol for Feminist Theology', *Concilium* 206 (1989), pp. 103-11.

J.R. Lundbom has published two rhetorical studies of passages in Hosea:
'Poetic Structure and Prophetic Rhetoric in Hosea', *VT* 29 (1979), pp. 300-308.
'Contentious Priests and Contentious People in Hosea IV 1-10', *VT* 36 (1986), pp. 52-70.

Indexes

Index of References

Old Testament

INDEX OF AUTHORS